D1215777

© 2016 by Leneita Fix
Published by Randall House
114 Bush Road
Nashville, TN 37217
www.randallhouse.com

Printed in the United States of America

ISBN-13: 978-0-89265-990-4

This book is dedicated to those I love beyond words. To my husband John, for choosing me, keeping me grounded in the midst of our "beautiful chaos," and for the constant reminder of what it means to belong to Christ. To Crystal, Caleb, Kaleigh and Bethany: I am grateful the Lord allows me to participate in your lives as you grow to be extraordinary men and women of God. To Jesus, without You I simply wouldn't be complete or know how to love my children, especially in these tumultuous adolescent years.

Introduction

You remember them. Years ago, they came—those zombie-like creatures who approached you out of nowhere. Dark circles accentuated drooping eyes and parched lips. Shoulders sagging, these "walking dead" types leered at your babies, toddlers, and preschoolers in tow and hissed, "Enjoy these years. One day, you'll have teenagers."

You laughed it off. "No, no, you don't understand. We just want to leave the house without diaper bags, strollers, and five changes of clothing. We'd like our kids to learn to put their shoes on all by themselves."

Cackling, they croaked, "Just. You. Wait." and they limped back into the shadows.

. . . . .

Then it happened. One day you woke up as the parent of tween- or teenagers. No one told you what these years would *really* be like. No one told you that no matter what choice you make, according to your teen, it's all wrong. No one told you your child will say things like, "I don't really need a parent anymore" as they run out, the door slamming behind them. No one mentioned you will do all the things "effective" parents of teens aren't supposed to do. In fact, you'll do all the things you said you'd never do. You'll give lectures standing with your hands on your hips. You'll lose your temper and say things like, "How many times have we been over this?"

No one warned you of the day your kids would be too old for you to fix a myriad of situations, from school to friends to frenemies. What about the moment you must tell your child that bullies are real and heartbreak comes in lots of flavors? There's also the first time your kids realize they really aren't good at something or someone throws the words "smart" around like an insult.

Part of you longs for the days when you could solve their

part of your daily life today to help ease you into the tumultuous years of raising teens. For those of us in the heat of the fire, these words are meant as a reassurance to keep going. Try some new approaches, and feel free to share some of yours with me. We're all learning together. None of us is perfect, and we must remember our kids don't belong to us but to the Lord. Through this book, I hope to help you find some times and ways to connect back to your children. You'll often read recurring words and themes, and I pray you will walk away with many practical helps as you travel alongside your kids on the journey toward adulthood.

I'll also use lots of examples from my children, Bethany, Caleb, and Kaleigh. However, you won't hear a lot about Crystal, our oldest. As I mentioned, she joined our family later in life, and out of respect to her extended family, I've chosen to focus on stories of my biological kids.

"Beauty in Action" sections at the end of each chapter provide interaction, questions, and steps you can use in your own family to apply what you've learned. And you may have heard the old saying, "How do you eat an elephant?" The answer, of course, is, "One bite at a time." Each chapter ends with "One Bite for Today," a small activity to help you connect with your kids.

When you see that young parent pushing a stroller down the street, dragging a toddler or two behind, please don't slink out of the shadows and cackle about the horror of the teen years. I promise: not only can we survive, but we can find ways to thrive—together.

–Leneita Fix

Chapter 1

"Excuse Me, Have We Met?"
When Your Baby Gets Eaten by Puberty

I never could have imagined how fast her huge blue eyes, strawberry blond hair, and rosy cheeks would capture my heart. We all love newborns, but we're all afraid to admit that most of them are homely. (We know it's true, but none of us wants to say it out loud.)

Bethany, our oldest, was the baby who immediately garnered oohs and ahhs, not only from family members (who felt obligated to say such things), but from strangers as well. Once when our little princess was about six months old, John and I left her with family for a date night at a restaurant. A couple sat next to us with their infant, and John decided he should go tell them how cute their baby was. When he returned, I asked, "Why did you do that?"

"Well, everyone always tells us how gorgeous Bethany is. I thought that's what you say to people who have babies."

"That's because Bethany *is* gorgeous. We don't have to lie."

Now before you judge me, let's admit it: no matter what anyone else says, we all believe our first is the most adorable child ever. Sure, people may have told us Bethany should have been a baby model, but chances are good someone told you something similar about your little one. We look at that precious face the first time it's covered in baby food and want to show the world. I filled roll upon roll of film with everything she did. In fact, we still have a mug emblazoned with a photo of her dressed as an angel for her first Christmas.

nerves. Those who once stood out from the crowd now had an unwavering need to fit in.

The puberty monster is devouring our kids, and we parents are at a loss. Sure, others had told us this day would come. And I genuinely thought I was ready. After all, I've spent the better part of twenty-four years pouring into teenagers in full-time ministry. When I'm not working with them directly, I'm writing resources for them or blogging about ways to better connect with them. In short, my whole career has been focused on helping teens and their parents.

I loved my own kids as babies, but I couldn't wait for the day they would get my jokes and want to sit and talk for hours about everything. Still, I was unprepared for just how unprepared I would be. The teen years were supposed to be our sweet spot. Instead, I found myself staring at my kiddos, trying to figure them out.

And talking to other parents with kids who were tweens and teens? That only made me feel worse. The overwhelming consensus was that we should just endure these years—put our heads down and soldier on through. For the time being, we should allow them to act like monsters, but one day our angelic creatures would return, and all would be right with the world.

· Those Were the Days ·

No one had told me it was natural to experience grief about the way our parenting changes course as our kids get older. One day I was complaining because all they wanted was to be held, and POOF the very next day I wished I could hold on to them for just a little longer. I didn't know I would stand in front of my children and say something like this, "Please be patient with me. You can't wait to grow up and get older. Yes there are parts that scare you, but overall I can tell this is exciting for you. For me, this is brand new, different and I'm not always sure I like it. I love you, and I'm here. Just know I don't and won't get it right all the time." Yes, I confess that to my kids often.

I had three children in two and a half years. When they were infants, toddlers, and preschoolers I was physically exhausted—yet the parenting felt more concrete. When they were hungry, we fed them. Tired? We put them to bed. When they acted out, we quickly told them how to readjust. And if they scraped a knee, we scooped them up in our arms and dried their tears with a cuddle.

The other day John and I were at the beach watching a dad play with his toddler. She would run into his arms where he would swing her upward, throw her high, catch her, and swoop her down. "Again! Again!" she squealed with glee. If this young father had allowed it, the game could have gone on for hours.

John and I both miss those days. As much as we longed for fewer tantrums and more sleep, back then, we felt like we had a grasp on what we were doing. Our hearts long for the connection we had with our babies along with the knowledge that we had many more years left to "get it right."

· Parents Anonymous? ·

When I hyperventilate at the thought of how little time there is left with my kids in my house, I also have to recognize the dread clinging to my soul. Anxiety washes over me. What if I mess up my kids to a point that will destroy them? What if they grow up to be failures—and I caused it?

We all have our definition of "parent fail." For some, it means our kids won't be successful in life without a solid education, good career, or financial stability. Others of us worry our children won't be happy. But, my biggest fear lingers in the back of my mind like a constant question: "What if my kids walk away from their relationship with the Lord and never come back?" Worse yet, "What if I'm the one who pushes them towards that choice?"

These fears are well-founded. I have good friends who are pastors or work in other areas of ministry whose children walked away from the faith. These were kids who, as teens, appeared to be on fire for the Lord. What will keep my kids from doing the same thing? John and I try to pray hard and do everything the Bible says, but what if it doesn't work?

This is the secret society of parents of adolescents. Welcome, here's your name tag and a cup of coffee. We're all sitting around believing we're the only ones who feel inadequate, while in truth, everyone else

In a an interview with the PBS show *Frontline*, Ellen Galinsky, president and founder of Families and Work, gives an interesting response to teens responding to their parents during these years. " If they pushed their parents away and their parents hung in there, they really appreciated it, because they knew that they were being difficult. That's the developmental task of the teen, to begin to separate from the parents in a new and different way. But it's also the developmental task of the teen to reconnect in a new way, in a more adult way. And so it's not just separation. We often thought of development as kind of a straight line toward independence. But all through development, there's separation and connection, and they go hand in hand." The bottom line is that the studies and statistics out there from organizations like the American Psychological Association prove that even when I'm doing it wrong, as a parent I have a greater influence than anyone else on the life of my child.[1] Psychologist Dr. Carl E Pickhardt, Ph.D., says it this way, "Parents vastly underestimate how closely they are observed and how constantly they are evaluated by their child."[2]

Sure, we should focus on character more deeply and tell them what's amazing about their talents, gifts, and soul. Yet, as the parent of three teens, I know when they look in the mirror they're not saying, "I look so compassionate today." Instead, they're acutely aware of the way their bodies have changed. They've forgotten they're created in the image of the Creator. I believe our role as parents is to keep taking the warped piece of looking glass out of their hands and help them see with the eyes of Christ. Perhaps this is the key to helping our kids grow into true disciples.

Even as they moan, I think we must keep posting pictures that celebrate them. Let's tell them their favorite shirt makes them look the opposite of whatever negative thought they have about themselves. The day we see on their face that they're happy with their looks, let's notice it. Even when they feel ugly, we as their parents realize they're not. Nope, they aren't babies anymore, but we're still glad they're our kids. We need to make sure they know it.

When I held that baby in the hospital, I was under the illusion that at eighteen, they would leave home, and my job would be done as a parent. Now as we enter the final stretch, I can see parenting just changes—it doesn't go away. It's time to settle in and keep at it. My child may look or act like the beast in fairy tales of old, but I need to remember the prince or princess underneath this rough exterior. At the same time, I have to keep reminding my beast of their true identity.

· Fear Not ·

I think the most helpful thing I need to remember is to stop panicking. Parenting out of an anxious place is rarely helpful. God put these kids in our homes for a reason. And that's true even on the days we look at them with utter confusion and have no idea how to figure them out. No matter how we feel in the moment, we're just the right parent for each of our children. Period.

I wish getting through these years was as simple as fixing a bad mood with a lollipop. Now, we must turn our face into the struggle and not give up. Each day we have to show up to be the parent, especially on the days we least want to. Remembering through it all God is bigger than any of us.

The only way I can avoid panicking and show up as a parent every day is to look to Him and His Word as a guide and keep filtering everything that way. I won't do it all correctly. I will mess up—again and again, and so will you. We must learn to tell our kids we're sorry and admit when we're wrong. We simply can't be perfect, no matter how much effort we put in. If we could, then let's face it, we wouldn't need a Savior.

Sometimes we need to let our kids try and fail, too. They'll make some choices we don't love. Yet, while they're growing, we can help them learn how to make better decisions. And we can lay down our disappointment when we let them learn.

It's gonna be all right. I promise. Let's dig in our heels, look forward, and remember God made pimple cream and tweezers. Sometimes we just have to be the ones to show our kids how to use them.

The older I get, the sicker roller coasters and spinning thrills make me. However, it doesn't mean I stop taking the ride. Parents, we have a choice: just survive these years or strap in for an adventure.

I'm in. Are you?

Beauty in ACTION

(This section will follow each chapter and is intended for use by individuals, couples, or groups as a means of reflecting on chapter contents and making application to your own life and parenting.)

1. Share three favorite memories from when your kids were little:

   a.

   b.

   c.

2. Name three ways your kids are struggling now that puberty has hit:

   a.

   b.

   c.

3. Describe two ways you can affirm your child today. (If you have more than one child, add answers for each one.)

a.

b.

4. List the top three fears you have about parenting during these years.

a.

b.

c.

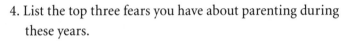

··· One Bite for Today ···

Try connecting with your child today to tell them why you love them. They need to hear those words often during these tumultuous years. In addition, tell them something you find amazing about them. It helps both of you to remember why they're extraordinary.

Chapter 2

The Core of Your Family: Standing Firm in Your Mission, Vision, and Values

We all do it. We live in the declarations of what our kids will "never do" before they actually arrive in our home. No television or sugar or fast food. Then one day you give in and buy the kids that first Happy Meal. Before you know it, your two year old is refusing to eat anything except McDonald's French fries. (Not that this happened to me.) You're still eating the words of "never do" when you opt for the bliss of plopping kids in front of two straight hours of *Dora the Explorer* to allow you the luxury of a shower and maybe even a rare bathroom break by yourself.

· Neverland ·

Shame overtakes us when our friend shares that she only allows her child to eat vegetables picked from their backyard garden. But, we can't get past the fact that the child eats the vegetable in the first place. When Bethany was about three, she would eat exactly one kernel of corn, get a look of pure disgust on her face, start gagging, and almost vomit across the table. Our reaction was simple: "You throw it up, you eat more corn." (I can't say I'm proud of that parenting practice.) To this day, when our kids don't like a food and get that look of distaste, we refer to it as "corn face."

So we make resolutions. We can eat at McDonald's, but only if you get the apple slices with your nuggets. Then one day those sad eyes move us to give in again. "French fries are made out of a distant relative of the potato, and that is a vegetable. But you may only have water or milk to drink." We do have our boundaries after all. And if you were one of those parents who could convince your children that peanut butter, raisins, and celery made a fun and nutritious snack of "ants on a log," more power to you. Mine looked at me and asked, "So you want me to eat bugs?"

· Different Strokes ·

I found as my kids started to head into adolescence the opinions of my peers became especially strong. It seemed everyone had an opinion about how to raise a healthy teen. Some of my friends took the "Let them do whatever" attitude. This group of parents believed the goal of adolescence was to allow your children to be exposed to everything the world had to offer. "If they're going to experience something, let them do it here first." This ran the gamut from movies to music to alcohol and everything in between.

Others took the opposite approach. Their kids weren't allowed to have anything to do with anything Mom and Dad believed was not of God. I remember when a sixth-grader told me, "I'm not allowed to listen to devil music." When I asked her what that meant, she told me, "Miley Cyrus." (Well, there were some wild years.) The ideas from this camp of parents took all sorts of interesting forms. Their teens couldn't watch movies that were too sexual, but their daughter donned a bikini at the beach. I had whiplash from all the people and opinions.

Chances are you've heard the words of Deuteronomy 6:5-9:

Love the Lord your God with all your heart and with all your soul and with all your strength. These commandments that I give you today are to be on your hearts. Impress them on your children. Talk about them when you sit at home and when you walk along the road, when you lie down and when you get up. Tie them as symbols on your hands and bind them on your foreheads. Write them on the doorframes of your houses and on your gates.

This is our rallying cry as parents. Yet in an era marked by instant access to media of all types, what does this passage mean for parents of kids ages nine through eighteen? When do we let them have a phone? Should my child use YouTube? What about Twitter, texting, and more?

As parents, we often feel like those "never"s keep creeping up on us. That book they could never read somehow ended up on their summer reading list. They somehow know all the words to the song they were never allowed to listen to. That movie we would never let them see is their cousin's favorite and of course they *had* to watch it together on a recent sleepover.

Take a deep breath. Right now. Right here.

· Relationship Goals ·

Parenting in the preteen and teen years begins with our own relationship with the Lord. The first step of the Deuteronomy 6 passage (and of parenting, period) is to fall in love with your Savior. We must come to grasp the great magnitude of what it means to belong to Jesus. Parenting is a lot less frightening when we rest in the knowledge that God is still caring for us as the best Dad ever. When we can take this in and let it sink into our hearts, then the rest is gravy, as they say. All right, maybe not gravy, but at least not as distressing.

Next, if we are to help our kids grow into successful adults, we must walk with them through these years. In every situation, we should be instilling what a relationship with Christ looks like and what it means to be His. This may have seemed simple when they were little, but today? Not so much. Notice that this passage does not tell us what video games our kids should play or whether or not we should deem the latest fashion craze appropriate.

This is why we must stop comparing ourselves to others. You're responsible for your family, period. You can only offer what you have—and that's an amazing thing.

· Personality Plus ·

I believe four elements make people who they are:

Nature: This is your personality, how God made you to be. Psalm 139:13-16 (NLT) says it well:

> *You made all the delicate, inner parts of my body and knit me together in my mother's womb. Thank you for making me so wonderfully complex! Your workmanship is marvelous—how well I know it. You watched me as I was being formed in utter seclusion, as I was woven together in the dark of the womb. You saw me before I was born. Every day of my life was recorded in your book. Every moment was laid out before a single day had passed.*

There are some characteristics you see early on in your children that reveal their personalities right away. Are they naturally shy, inquisitive, or funny? Think about yourself in high school. Which qualities still describe you today? Are you quick-witted? Outgoing? Congenial—just as you were back then? This, my friend, is your personality.

Do we need to allow the Lord to take our personality and mold it? Of course. However, some core elements of our identity will never change. Knowing Bethany needs time to process has helped me understand her better. When she has something important to tell us, she often struggles to find the best time to share it. As a result, when she wants to talk, she'll stare at me, often giving other cues in her body language such as taking a deep breath. She usually waits for me to say something along the lines of "Do you have something you would like to talk about?"

This is her unique personality. Someday she will mature into understanding how to start these conversations, but her need to process and chew on a thought is a part of who she is and will always be.

Nurture: This is the way we are brought up and all the ways the various situations in our upbringing affected us. Malcolm Gladwell in his book *Outliers: The Story of Success* makes a profound statement: "We overlook just how large a role we all play—and by 'we' I mean society—in determining who makes it and who doesn't."[3] You may have one child who was bullied and another who wasn't. Those elements of their lives, positive or negative, that we can't change but that change us, serve as the nurturing elements in our lives.

Choices: We land in a variety of situations where we truly do choose our own path. You ask your child to clean their room, and they choose whether to obey or disobey. Either path has a consequence attached. Child development experts argue about nature and nurture and whether they work against each other; however, our choices, including the depth of our relationship with Christ, also play a huge role in the way our lives go.

Development: Erik Erikson was a psychologist and psychoanalyst who identified eight stages through which a healthy, developing human should pass from infancy to late adulthood. In his stages of physiological development, children in elementary school (ages five through twelve) are influenced most by their relationship with parental figures, neighbors, and teachers.[4] They start to ask themselves, "Can I make it in this world of people and things?"

This shifts late in the twelfth year, and by the time they reach ages thirteen through nineteen, they start to put more emphasis on their relationships with peers and role models. They ask, "Who am I? Who can I be?" In other words, adolescence is marked by a child's desire to fit in and find themselves.

Up to this point, a child is shaped by what is done to them. As they mature, they make more and more decisions about who they are and what they want to be. In contrast, those of us in our thirties and forties are asking, "Can I love?" and, "Can I make my life count?" We have strong attachments to our households, friends, and coworkers.[5] Thus our stage of development is far different than the stage in which our kids find themselves.

If we put this all together it looks like this:

Nature + Nurture + Choices + Development = Perspective

· Super Bowl ·

I can't compare myself to you because we look at the world in vastly different ways. And each child will be different, too. The way you and I walk out that passage from Deuteronomy 6 will carry the same truth but look different in each family and for each child.

For example, my son is extremely compassionate and sensitive. If you say to him, "Hey, could you go brush your teeth? I think you forgot," he's likely to believe he's a horrible person with the worst breath ever.

My youngest, on the other hand, is in no danger of oversensitivity. Actually, she seems to have no filter at all. Yeah, she's that kid who often says out loud what we're all thinking. If it enters her brain, it comes out of her mouth.

These and other personality differences mean John and I have to approach each of our children entirely differently. I've only shared small snippets about their personalities. But put these three together with a child who became part of our family when she was in high school, along with all their parents' quirks, and we start to look like Fruit Loops that have been left in their milk a little too long. All the flavors and colors bleed together, but it's our own bowl of cereal. You have yours. There's no way you can duplicate what we do, nor should you.

· Reality Check ·

I'll admit it: our family has always been a little different. I've heard it said that in a marriage relationship, one is a racehorse always trying to see how fast they can take the track, while the other is the plow horse: calm, deliberate, and methodical. Ninety percent of the time when we meet couples who are in ministry, the husband is the racehorse. Not in our home. I am totally trying to pull ahead while John is saying, "Slow and steady wins the race."

During one season of our ministry, I received harsh criticism about my role as wife and mother. The hurt was so great that all I could do was seek the Lord on how to handle the situation well, asking Him if I needed to change the way I approached both marriage and parenting. One day, John looked at me and declared, "I'm not unhappy. I think you're a great wife and mom. If God and I are OK with you, then let's stop listening to the naysayers."

At that point, we put in place a system of checks and balances. Before we make decisions that affect our family, we ask the following questions:

Are we sinning?
Are we walking out of the will of God?
Will this hurt us or others?
Will we all be miserable?

Notice we don't ask if our decision will make *anyone* unhappy. We will always have decisions we must make as parents that will upset someone in the mix. But if the decision makes the entire family miserable, we might need to make an adjustment in attitude, approach, or circumstances.

Once we came to embrace the family God has called us to be, a deep peace settled in. Knowing your family identity helps both parents understand and agree with where your children and your family are going. I understand that families have changed, and you may or may not live with your child's other biological parent. Yet, the more you as parents can discuss and attempt to agree on some common ground, the more you and your adolescent will understand what you expect.

· Back to the Future ·

Understanding expectations also explains the importance of praying about the kind of adults you want your children to become. You may have heard the statement, "Begin with the end in mind."[6] But what does that mean? It's easy to think "the end" means going to college, participating on a sports team, or playing a musical instrument. All of those things are important. But those are all things your children will do—not who they will be. How often do we pray about the person we want them to be when they are out of our home, living as adults? What does the whole person—emotionally, physically, and spiritually—look like to both parents?

I will give you few formulas in this book. Most of the time, I'll share ideas and suggestions instead. But we can get overwhelmed when we try to juggle the multiple perspectives and questions involved in looking ahead. Even if we have an idea about the person we'd like our child to become one day, how do we put it all together? My husband and I have identified four pieces to a system that can help. The first is to make sure you have a family mission statement: one sentence that sums up who your family is and what you are about. It should be easy to remember and something your children can easily repeat. Ours is simple: Love Christ, Serve Others. The foundation of our family is to love and be loved by Jesus. When we understand how much He loves us, all we will want is to give that love away. The next piece is to choose three core values that guide your family—unwavering principles that define you. In other words, if your children walk out the door knowing nothing else, they will have taken these values to heart. Ours are integrity, servant leadership, and being Christ-centered. It's not that other values aren't important, but for us, these are essential. Your family's core values might be faithfulness, hard work, or something else, but whatever they are, take intentional time to sit down and figure them out. What principles do you keep teaching your kids over and over? Identifying those areas should give you a head start on selecting your core values.

Third, *choose one Bible verse that belongs to your whole family.* We used ours in our wedding, and it has been the center of who we are ever since. It is Jeremiah 29:11-13: "'For I know the plans I have for you,' declares the Lord, 'plans to prosper you and not to harm you, plans to give you hope and a future. Then you will call on me and come and pray to me, and I will listen to you. You will seek me and find me when you seek me with all your heart.'" What verse defines your family? What do you take to heart more than any other?

Finally, go back and, with the first three pieces in place, *ask the Lord what He wants your kids to look like when they leave your home.* Spend time praying and in the Word (together if possible) and allow Him to show you what His greatest desire is for your children. Through this process, John and I have come to long for our kids to be adults who are fully-devoted followers of Jesus. We want them to have a faith that outshines ours. Again, that may be easy to say, but what does it look like in a practical sense?

To answer this question, we made a list. Part of it contains attributes that appear when someone truly belongs to the Lord. Looking at Biblical examples, mentors, friends, and family we brainstormed characteristics we see in those who have long-term vibrant relationships with Christ. David was a man after God's own heart. Joshua and Caleb believed God keeps His promises when others did not. Paul reminds us what it means to be used by Christ in a mighty and humbling way. Our friend Pastor Steve is compassionate and faithful. My grandmother Leneita was tenacious in the way she cared for forgotten people. Our list includes words like: integrity, servant-leader, bold faith, humility, compassion, and love. The other half holds practical skills we want to make sure our kids can handle before they leave our home. Some of these are spiritual disciplines like prayer or alone-time with God. Others will help them manage a household, like budgeting, cooking, and caring for others.

Our list helps us parent with greater intentionality, especially in these final years together. Our kids will leave home knowing how to do laundry, clean a toilet, tithe, work hard, have alone-time with God, and serve others. What does your list look like?

Once you have these elements in place, stick to your convictions. You have your mission, values, Scripture, and vision. But this isn't a method or system designed to keep all issues or problems away. Again, if we could design (or live by) a perfect formula, we wouldn't need Jesus.

Talk to God continually about your children. Allow Him to guide you all along the way. At this point in your childrearing, you may have defined these elements but never taken time to write them down. Get them on paper (or on a backed-up file in your computer) now.

Of course, you'll still experience rocky patches. But often, the rough places help John and me realize when we've been making decisions that don't fit our family identity. Identifying our core values and principles keeps everyone building momentum together as we move toward the same goals.

What about you and your family?

(I promise: this is the most work I will require at the end of any chapter. But when you take the time to put this all together, it will help you understand who you are and move your family forward.)

1. Nature: Name three truths about your personality:

   a.

   b.

   c.

2. Name one event (good or bad) in your life that helped make you who you are today:

3. List two choices you made that have affected your life.

   a.

   b.

3. Write your family mission statement here:

4. Write your family core values here:

5. Write your family Scripture passage here:

6. Write a brief summary of the vision God has given you for your children here:

···One Bite for Today···

This chapter required a lot of thinking and working as a family. But none of these steps will have any impact if you don't put them into action. Once you've listed your mission, vision, values, and Scripture in the steps above, type them up and put them where your family can see them. Refer to them often and make sure your children know exactly what they mean. Your family needs to see you living out these values day by day.

Chapter 3

Opening Thoughts on Communicating with Our Kids

Communication seemed easier when our kids were young, or maybe the pressure to connect wasn't as prevalent back then. But now, we've started the countdown clock.

When our children are babies, we love to count up as they grow. We think we may not survive the toddler years, full of biting and tantrums. Then, as a friend of mine likes to say, we hit the "sweet years" of kindergarten through third grade. Our children chat with us, ask us questions, and want to come to us with their problems. They curl up with us on the couch, still want to be tucked in at night and talk about their dreams and fears.

Then, almost overnight, our kids seem to shut down. This is when the countdown begins to play around at the back of our mind. No longer are we anticipating our children growing older. Instead, we're watching the numbers fly as the amount of time that remains before they leave grows smaller and smaller. One night, we wake up in a cold sweat as we realize that the clock is ticking wildly out of control. In the midst of busy schedules, hormones, and a roller coaster of emotions, we long for them to talk to us, yet it feels like we no longer know how to communicate. I experienced this recently while sitting at a red light when Caleb blurted out something that stirred deep emotions in me. It wasn't exactly anger that had boiled to the surface. No, this feeling was something different. It was exasperation. I breathed my current go-to prayer, "Lord, please teach me how to talk to these kids during this season of their lives. I have no idea what to say anymore."

You see, it often feels like it doesn't matter what words come out of my mouth, because they're wrong. All wrong. I might as well spill alphabet soup on the table and read whatever shows up. That would be just as accurate in reaching my children during these teen and pre-teen years. The old days of "Brush your teeth before bed," or "Eat all your vegetables if you want dessert." are so over.

Recently I heard Phil Vischer, creator of the animated series *Veggie Tales*, speak at a conference.[7] Many of his words worked their way into my soul, including this concept: "We underestimate what kids can learn, and we overestimate what adults are interested in."

By way of example, he told us when children are small, they ask, "Why is the sky blue?" Adults rarely ask that question, but not because the masses have learned the science behind our blue sky. Most of us have simply ceased to wonder about it.

This is a beautiful representation of our current phase of parenting. Our adolescent kids are making the transition from wondering about everything to keeping their thoughts to themselves. I believe this is why parents of teens find communication so difficult. The rules have changed in our own homes. All of a sudden, our kids expect us to read their minds, and when we can't figure out what they're thinking, they get frustrated.

· Breakdown ·

I admit it: yesterday I broke down in front of my kids. Tears rolled down my cheeks because I wanted to communicate well but couldn't. Somehow, I hadn't figured out that one child did indeed want to go to the birthday party an old friend invited her to, the other did not want to go to the mall to run errands, and still another child was having self-esteem issues. Since I failed to read all the signs correctly, I said, "All right, everyone, get your shoes on. It's time to leave."

The gnashing of teeth and writhing on the floor that ensued gave me a clue that I could have said this in a better way. But I was tired of trying to figure it out, and the constant need to get it right exhausted me.

So here we stood with everyone angry, and I started to cry. "I want to do this right. I just don't always know how I am supposed to talk to you. Some days I can't figure out what you're thinking without you actually saying it out loud." I paused to blow my nose. "I must have missed the secret code somewhere. I don't always know there are deeper issues to running errands than running errands. Could you help me out sometimes and use your words instead of being frustrated when I don't even know why?" Another pause and a deep breath. "Do you know how hard it is to try to keep everyone happy? I mean, I know it's not my job to make you happy, but do you know how hard it is to figure you all out and know when I am and am not supposed to talk to you?"

They stared at me blankly as my sobs came harder. Then *their* tears flowed. "I'm sorry I made you cry," one of them gulped.

"I'm sorry for breaking down," I pulled it together enough to say.

"We're sorry for being unresponsive," one said as the others nodded.

"Let's start over." That seemed to work for everyone.

This is the dance of communicating with our kids. We all have to remember we're learning it together. The game is changing, the clock is ticking, yet we're still on the same team (even when it feels like we're all playing different sports at the same time.)

· Out of Control ·

All the components of personalities, experiences, and choices play a huge role in how our children want to interact with us. In addition, they have insecurities, fears, and growing pains that make them choose to interact with us differently than with one another. This is why we often label one child "easier" than others.

The truth is, some of our kids want to talk about everything all the time. Some want to talk as long as they choose the topic and avoid hard issues. Still others play a game of cat and mouse, hoping we'll figure them out. I learned just recently I can get far more out of my youngest when she is texting than in a face-to-face conversation. Finally, there are those who need to process what they're saying, so every conversation is ordered and intentional.

But no matter how your kids react, twenty-four years in ministry and seventeen as a parent have taught me this: when it comes to communicating with them, our kids don't want us to give up. They need us to engage, press in, and try our best—even when we get it wrong. The issue, of course, that I will bring up over and over throughout these pages is that the whole process is exhausting—not just the parenting but the communicating. We want our kids to meet us on our turf, where we can call the shots. They want us to meet them on their turf, where they have control. But talking to our kids is not about control at all. Instead, it's about deepening our relationship.

· Listen Up ·

Life gets busy, and meeting our kids in the way they prefer can be excruciating. The countdown clock I mentioned can get lost in all the places we need to go and all the things we need to accomplish in a day. I don't think we disengage intentionally, though. The communication gap widens slowly until, all of a sudden, something jostles us awake. Maybe we realize we haven't had an intentional conversation about the facts of life, dating, drugs, or choices in general. Maybe we hear a speaker or watch a special on television that leaves us saying, "I need to get on top of that. I only have a short time left."

We end up with a tendency to corner our kids and, using our most serious tone of voice, speak the dreaded words, "We have to talk." This, of course, goes horribly awry because we blush or stutter or seem to get the words out incorrectly. And our teens get embarrassed, shut down, or at best stare straight through us. These reactions are natural for them, but for us, almost every conversation feels like an episode of *Mission: Impossible*. We just want them to hear the right information and take it to heart.

Some days, communication feels like we're not talking *to* our children but *at* them instead. As we become impassioned about who we want to see them become, we watch their eyes glaze over. I've learned that although kids of this age may not say a word, they do take what we say to heart.

Years ago, in an exasperated moment with the youth group I ran, I blurted out, "Do you guys even listen to what I'm saying?" One of the students gave a response I still remember. "Mrs. Leneita, we're always listening. Sometimes we just like to pretend we aren't."

If this is true of a youth group, how much more so of our own kids?

· Parent Trap ·

A few years ago, I decided to lead my youth group in a six-week series about connecting with their parents. Since Scripture says to honor our parents (not if they're good, worthy, or awesome—just honor them) I thought it might be wise to help students interact with the people they live with. The first week, I gave them a challenge, "You have to spend thirty minutes with your parents this week. You can do it all at once or split it up over the next seven days. The only requirement is that you're not allowed to wait for your parents to interact with you. You have to go to them. It might feel awkward. That's all right. Get beyond the feeling and just give it a try."

The students glared at me in disbelief, but I made sure to let them know I would ask about their interactions the following week and offered a small prize to anyone who remembered their homework. These students came from all sorts of backgrounds with a variety of parental situations: single parents, two-parent households, and grandparents raising grandchildren.

The next week, I didn't have to ask how it went. Students clamored to share their stories of walking into the kitchen and starting conversations with their mom or asking if they could spend some time with a dad. The immediate, skeptical reaction of each adult was, "Do you want something? What are you looking for?" Not one of them believed their children would just want to talk.

Some of the students told their parents it was part of an assignment. Most did not. But over and over again, the students told me they now felt closer to their parents and would try to do this more often. They had actually enjoyed chatting with their parents. Go figure. I remember one young man who sat on the couch and watched a movie with his father. For the first fifteen minutes, his dad kept asking if he needed something, and the son kept repeating, "No, I just want to watch this with you." It didn't take long for the dad to engage with his boy, and before either one realized it, two hours had passed.

I'll never forget the young man's words: "I'm glad I did that."

· Press On ·

It sometimes feels like our teens and preteens only want us to shuttle them from one activity to the next, make sure they're clothed and fed, drop forgotten items off at school, and be around to help in the case of a heart- or stomach-ache. We tend to believe that because communication between us has changed, our kids don't want to hear from us anymore, so we back off. But they do want us—much more than we realize. I keep coming across articles that explain why teens don't talk to their parents anymore. In *The Huffington Post* author Kate Russell claims it is usually not because parents are uncaring, instead "The problem, it seemed, stemmed from their childhood, where somewhere along the way, they had come to the conclusion that their parent's love and approval was conditional and based on good behavior and achievement."[8] Last night when I asked if Kaleigh needed help in science because she struggled with a recent test, she accused me of being mad at her. I explained I really just wanted to make sure she wasn't struggling, which uncorked the real issue. She doesn't feel like she is good at anything except school these days. I might say to Ms. Russell's claim, sometimes our children misconstrue our expectations, and make themselves believe we don't want them unless they are "good enough." On the other hand I also have come upon numerous top 10 lists of things teens wished their parents knew about them. They are written from parenting experts and bloggers. I am not sure where all of the information comes from but they all say something in them about our kids listening to us, and wanting us to ask about their days. They say things like, "I wish my parents wouldn't assume what I like, but would ask me about my interests." In a *Psychology Today* article,[9] or "Adolescents who are strongly connected to their parents perform better in school and are less likely to smoke, abuse drugs and engage in other destructive behaviors. Even if you feel you've lost all influence, keep talking—your teens are listening," according to Aspen Education Group.[10]

Family and Work Institute founder Ellen Galinsky (who I have mentioned previously) was interviewed by *Frontline* a number of years ago about a study she had conducted with 1,023 children ages 8-18. She claims that we parents believe we know what's going on in our children's lives, while they believe we don't. On the other hand when asked if teens want more time with their parents, she had this to say, "I found a big surprise, which is that it was teens more than younger children who felt that they didn't have enough time with their parents. And in one sense, it makes sense, because parents of teens spent a lot less time with their teenagers than parents of younger children do. So you can see that there's a difference in the amount of time spent so, yes, OK, they want more time."[11] Teens act like they want independence, but this doesn't mean they don't want to have our time, thoughts, opinions, or guidance. Instead, what they want from our conversations has shifted. Now, they look to us less for direction or commands and more for coaching.

Remember the verses from Deuteronomy 6 we discussed in the first chapter? It's easy to read this or other familiar passages for parents and think, "Yes, yes, I know." But let's remember that we haven't finished this task yet. Proverbs 1:8–9 flips the "teach them diligently" idea on its head: "Listen, my son, to your father's instruction and do not forsake your mother's teaching. They are a garland to grace your head and a chain to adorn your neck." When we combine the two passages, we are given the charge to ensure we love the Lord with everything we have, so we seek Him and share

His truth with our kids. Our children, then, will take what we say, listen to it, and allow it to fill them up.

Even the New Testament directs our kids to listen and follow: "Children, obey your parents in the Lord, for this is right. 'Honor your father and mother'—which is the first commandment with a promise—'so that it may go well with you and that you may enjoy long life on the earth'" (Eph. 6:1–3).

I'd love it if this were simple. But the next verse shows us the difficulty: "Fathers, do not exasperate your children; instead, bring them up in the training and instruction of the Lord" (Eph. 6:4). There it is again, the reminder that our lives well-lived with Christ at the center matters in how we raise our kids. They will learn from watching us, even when we fall down. As my husband often says, "It isn't if we mess up that always matters, what matters is how we deal with the mess up."

· Love Languages ·

How our kids seek out communication with us, I believe, has its roots in both personality and love languages. In case you're not familiar with *The Five Love Languages*, let me explain. Dr. Gary Chapman came up with this means of describing the different ways we give and receive love. He says the primary way we express love is also the way we want to receive it.

Here's a quick synopsis of the five he claims are the most prevalent. *Words of affirmation* are verbal and written praise and affirmation. If this is your love language, harsh words hurt you deeply, and you love handwritten letters, notes, quotes, and verbal expressions of love. The bedroom walls of my child who favors this love language are covered with favorite quotes, Scripture, and song lyrics. In their world, sending a simple text message that says, "YOU ARE BREATHTAKING and I love you just because God made you" is huge.

Acts of service are expressions of help and practical service. For these people, actions truly do speak louder than words. To show love to a child with this primary love language, you can clean their bedroom or help with a school project.

Receiving gifts is the third love language, and the one that speaks to me a hundredfold. No, it's not about something expensive or fancy, but "the thought that counts."

One of my favorite presents ever was a pair of socks my best friend sent me from England. Twenty years ago, when she was my college roommate, I said I would love to collect socks with sheep on them. Over two decades, this has amounted to about four pairs of socks. But on a recent birthday, I opened a box to find a cute pair of sheep socks. My children thought I was crazy as I laughed, cried, and screamed all at once. I didn't love the footwear as much as I loved the way my friend remembered something so small but true. Every present that has mattered to me over the years has been because the person thought of me when they purchased it.

Physical touch is the fourth love language. For a person with this as their primary way of giving and receiving love, intentional hugs or hand-holding spell love.

The final love language is *quality time*, which is much more than just being together. The person who favors this love language wants to feel like they matter to their loved one more than anyone else in the room.

According to Dr. Chapman, each person leads with two of the five. I believe these love languages make a huge difference in the way families communicate. Over and over again, our adolescents need to hear they are loved, but we have to say it in a multitude of ways. What this means is that we must learn to communicate with each of our kids differently. One may want to talk about everything, to spend time with you just to chat face to face. Another may need to go do something alongside you in order to be drawn out. For still another merely sitting close to her and stroking her hair with no words at all can undo a bad day.

We need to keep reassuring our kids that we want to hear from them while communicating "I love you" in a way they understand best.*[12] It takes some extra thought and effort to think through how to best approach each child, but the results will be worth it.

At the same time, we have to take the pressure off ourselves to get every conversation right. I'm learning that just showing up and trying makes a difference. And sometimes my kids don't want to go deep. They just want to be silly, which is equally valuable. Getting our kids to be goofy, share their favorite movie, or talk about something stupid they saw today reminds us how to connect. I have to reassure myself often that the act of conversation matters more than its topic.

· Photo Op ·

Photographer Eric Pickersgill offered an interesting look at our society. He took pictures of people in social settings as they held mobile technology. Then he removed the devices from their hands, asking them to keep the same pose and expression as he snapped more photos. His shots revealed people near each other without interacting, their hands poised as if holding phones, but empty.

Two of the most interesting shots showed a mother and daughter next to each other on the couch, touching each other while staring down at their hands, and the other was a family around the dinner table, close to each other but not interacting. Sometimes we think we're communicating only because we're near our kids. John and I often realize that we've spent time near our children for several days in a row but haven't actually talked with them. Sitting with our kids and putting technology away so we can connect is powerful. Whenever we can, we sit across from our kids and look them in the eye. This seems disarming at first but creates a connection that allows for open dialogue.[13]

In the end, we need to remember that our kids want us. They want our love, and they want for us to truly know who they are and what they are going through. They need us. We just have to be willing to do the work to keep communicating even when they act like they don't want to. There's a push and pull, try and fail. It's all right when you fall down or mess up—that happens. Apologize. Keep showing up in the conversation. And stop looking at the countdown clock. Our kids may leave home, but they won't stop talking to us—as long as we do the work to keep the conversation going.

1. What stands out to you about what the Bible says about communication with our children?

2. In what ways has your communication with your kids changed as they've matured?

3. Name a time you and your kids struggled to communicate. How did you respond?

4. Make a list of everyone who lives in your house and their love languages here.

···One Bite for Today···

Remember that continuing to try is vital. Invite your kids to sit with you and begin by asking about their days. Tell them you love them in a way that matters to them.

Chapter 4

My Life as A Chauffeur:
Minivans Happen to the Best of Us

I didn't own a car until I was twenty-four years old. When I finally got one, I thought I was pretty cool because it was a used '87 Nissan Pulsar sports car with T-tops. (I think I paid $3,000 total for it.) Then I grew up a little into a small four-door sedan for a brief period before I had three babies in two and a half years. We outgrew that car, and the next logical choice was a minivan.

· Time for a Change ·

It's happened to all of us parents: the moment when the car we want becomes a distant memory as we move to the car the family needs.

I could explain how the minivan is worth it and that trading in my dream vehicle for a van full of strollers, football equipment, backpacks, and crayon stains never made me look back. But I just watched a Jeep Wrangler drive by and found myself wondering, "Do we really need to fit our whole family into one vehicle?"

Please do not tell me the minivan is awesome. Whenever I lament about mine, someone inevitably tells me how much they love the functionality or storage. So why do so many of us mourn the day we get stuck in the proverbial parent mobile? (Yours may not even be an actual minivan, but if you are in any vehicle you would not choose sans children you catch my drift.) Sure, I've seen the funny videos that refer to our minivans as "swagger wagons." But in reality, driving a minivan marks the end of the swagger era. The days of allowed irresponsibility are over. Instead, the minivan announces the era in which you apologize to friends for the stinky mess of your vehicle as you wipe crushed Cheerios off the place they had hoped to sit. It symbolizes the realization that selfishness is no longer allowed. Making decisions about our needs and our desires is more fantasy than reality.

However, I wouldn't trade my minivan, because uncool as it is, it represents a season of my life that won't last forever. I often tell new parents, "The moment you meet your child is the moment you can't remember a time without them." Whether they enter your life through birth or adoption, they take over your world, and you can't imagine it any other way.

We'll always have days when we wish we could make a choice with no one else in mind. But then we remember the little people that occupy our thoughts almost every minute, and our sacrifices come naturally. Some people call this "dying to self." I prefer to see it as unconditional love and the recognition that we're all in this together. But we have to practice it every day. The minivan or family car says to our kids, "You're worth it."

· Now You're Talking ·

Our minivan no longer smells of forgotten sippy cups with week-old milk on a hot summer's day. However, it does stink of old cleats and perfume. Somewhere along the way, I had a revelation. Our minivan is a central place of conversation for my kids. The older they've become, the more time we spend driving from one activity or event to the next. Those years before they have a license or a car are invaluable. In one afternoon, I often have three different pick-ups and drop-offs. One has volleyball until 4:30; the next, cheer practice until 5:30; and then football ends at 6:30. Our kids also have jobs, voice lessons, photography, after-school help, and Saturday practices. When they're not in the car, I use that time to pray, worship, and even sit in silence. Seriously, there are days when five minutes in that minivan is the only alone- or off- time I have. Can you relate?

There are a few reasons the minivan becomes a great place to talk, especially about tough topics. First of all, a van ride usually takes a definitive amount of time from start to finish. The second reason may sound creepy but I have found it to be true. In a car ride our kids are stuck with us, and have a few short moments where they have no place else to be except in that seatbelt. My kids go to a school that doesn't provide bus service, so we drive them back and forth. That twenty minutes to and from school has been a gold mine. I can ask about their days, friends, and situations they encounter. Over the years, our kids have also looked to time in the car as time to chat about topics they fear might take too long to explain. Even a five-minute ride to the store can prove a treasure trove of communication.

The lack of eye contact is another reason both parent and child appreciate a minivan trip. The other day, I was invited to teach at an assembly at my kids' high school. I did my best not to embarrass them by acknowledging them as they sat with their friends, sharing stories about our home life, or pointing to them as examples. In the van on the way home, I asked, "How'd I do?"

My son confessed, "When you started, your jokes were so corny I was worried, but I was thankful it got better." Yep, that's who I am. Just on the other side of cool, yet I was glad for his candor. And I don't know that it would have happened without the van ride.

· That Was Awkward ·

But the impromptu minivan conversations don't work to my advantage when they force me to face life's awkward conversations. The times I set aside for "the talk" are OK—because I've prepped, read up, and thought ahead for questions. But no one prepares us for the times these conversations just happen. You know, like the time your husband's away on a business trip and your tween son's friends at school uses a sexual euphemism he doesn't understand, and he decides to ask you what it means. Yes, that time.

Your mind reels, wondering what's enough and what's too much information while his sisters sit in the back seat. As you explain, his jaw drops, and one sister screams, "Ewwwwwwwww" while the other puts her fingers in her ears, yelling, "I can't hear you!"

At the next red light, you find yourself wildly texting your husband, "SO NOT FAIR. DO YOU KNOW WHAT I HAD TO ANSWER JUST NOW? COME HOME!"

But I'm grateful that through the stutters, beads of sweat, and bright red cheeks, my children are still asking us questions. They trust John and I will share the best answer we can give. I think they also appreciate our admission of our awkwardness in these sensitive topics. I've told my kids, "I might blush, but it doesn't mean I won't talk to you about it."

Remember, though, that we don't need to give all the details from our personal experiences as they ask questions. It's OK to take a moment and to regroup. Just don't stop answering. Yes, it's uncomfortable and awkward and strange to answer the taboo topics. But I would much rather be the one to try to tell them than some twenty year old who posts naughty pictures on the Internet. Most of the time, parent and child are both glad these can happen within the confines of that safe little box that allows for unscripted moments. So create a space where your kids feel comfortable telling you their thoughts.

· Expert Opinion? ·

Somehow, we parents continue under the illusion that we're supposed to be experts on every topic. We may send our kids to others because we think we can't figure out what to tell them. And this is probably the number-one conversation I have with other parents of kids who are at that junior high and high school age. "I feel so inadequate," we all say. Sure we know that we should be the ones they turn to for hard conversations, especially about their relationship with Jesus; however, we aren't theologians. I remember a few years ago, my husband and I had dinner at the home of some friends. Their children were good friends with our kids and all were between the ages of twelve and fourteen. This couple seemed like perfect parents who seemed to have all the answers to every question—and they had perfect kids, too.

I remember sitting in the car with John later that day as we discussed the evening and wondered if we were doing everything wrong. We were doing our best. We prayed for our kids and kept pointing them back to Jesus as the center of their lives, but we weren't these people. The next day as we drove somewhere, I don't recall the question, but I remember having an in-depth conversation with my kids about their faith. I think I even had them look up some answers in their Bibles as we drove.

A few weeks later, I looked down our row at church to see all of my kids worshipping in ways that showed their deep love for the Lord. It was at this moment I realized all these conversations are vital. We don't need to be experts in Hebrew, Greek, apologetics, theology or biblical definitions. But we do need to keep seeking the Lord with our whole hearts, learning daily what it means to be His, and then passing along everything we learn. More often than not, these deep questions come within the walls of the minivan.

· The Big Dorito ·

Caleb had to be about three or four at the time. Although that was almost a decade ago, I can still recall the moment as if it were yesterday. He sat in his car seat behind John, covered in the nacho cheese goodness that comes with the best snack foods. He has always been our most inquisitive child, and this day was no exception, as his questions came fast and furious. The first few were easy (sort of). "Why is the sky blue?" "What makes grass grow?" "How do they get the cream in the middle of a Twinkie?" Then he dropped one of those questions every parent dreads, the ones you have to think about and are still pondering yourself: "If Jesus loves everyone, then why doesn't everyone get to go to Heaven to be with Him forever?"

I looked at John. He looked at me. Our minds spun through theology, Scripture, and opinion. Time seemed to move in slow motion as we put our thoughts in some sort of order so we could answer our preschooler. For that twenty seconds, we felt frozen. John opened his mouth. "Well, buddy . . ."

"Daddy! Look at the size of this Dorito!" Caleb squealed with delight. The moment was gone. Had we taken too long to answer? Was disaster averted, or should we revisit the question? Our son looked out the window and began to jabber about clouds and their shapes. He had indeed moved on.

Ever since, we refer to some questions as "The Big Dorito." There are times when your children are struggling to understand. They grapple with their faith and who Christ is. Other times, they ask a question only because it entered their mind. And just as quickly, they move on to the next thing. Caleb still does this as a teen—all of my kids do. It's important to treat every question as important, but also to discern when they want to know the answer and when they only want to ask.

· Test Drive ·

When we work to keep the space open for discussion in the car, it can become a hub of activity. I confess that as much as it is a place of constant chatter, there are times when both parents and teens prep for car-ride conversations. Some kids will save an important conversation for an upcoming car ride. With others, you may have to ask open-ended questions to avoid constant "Yes" or "No" answers. And do make sure to schedule rides with just one parent and one teen. We've used times like this to combat insecurity with truth, discuss needed attitude adjustments, and to just get to know our kids better.

The car is the perfect place to learn our kids—their likes and dislikes, joys, fears, and concerns. Try some stupid-but-creative questions (and don't be afraid to answer them too.) After school, I love to ask, "What's the craziest thing that happened today?" And some of my favorite car conversations are about nothing at all, just silly moments where the kids are clamoring to share a thought. We've had deep talks on what would happen in the event of a zombie apocalypse, our favorite superhero, and whether or not the cheese in Kraft Macaroni & Cheese can actually be considered a dairy product. During these times of tuning in and joining the silliness, I hear my kids share those insane thoughts no one wants to say out loud. These are great times. Don't miss them.

Beauty in ACTION

1. What's the most fun you've ever had in the family car?

2. Name one "Big Dorito" moment in your car ride.

3. List three silly questions that might help you get to know your kids better. (Example: "If you were a kitchen utensil, what would you be and why?")

    a.

    b.

    c.

4. What's one time you have felt inadequate when answering a question in the car?

5. Write out one question you can spend some time prepping for in case it comes up in the car.

··· One Bite for Today ···

This week, take the time to have one unscripted and one scripted conversation with each of your children. In the unscripted one, pay attention to a conversation that gets started in the car and jump in. For the scripted one, plan out one conversation you would like to have with your child this week. It doesn't have to be a tough topic. Just think about something you might like to know and ask some questions.

Please note: If you haven't made these practices part of your everyday relationship quite yet, it may feel awkward. That's all right. Let your kids stare. Just start talking and don't be afraid of strange pauses. The momentum will build. Just keep trying.

Chapter 5

Daily Rituals: Using Everyday Moments for Deeper Communication

D
o you remember "The More You Know," campaign of public service announcements that NBC broadcast a few years back? It usually involved a celebrity of some kind giving brief information about a critical topic and ended with an animated star sweeping across the screen with the tagline, "The More You Know."

· Table Talk ·

I recall one of these many years ago that focused on the importance of the family dinner table. As I was trying to find this PSA in the archives of search engines, I came across an entire nonprofit dedicated to promoting the idea of families eating around the table together. The co-founder of The Family Dinner Project, Anne K. Fishel, has also authored an entire book on taking back mealtimes. She contends that the actual meal doesn't matter; it can be breakfast or Sunday brunch instead. There's no magic number for mealtime meetings, although at least five a week is preferable. Family mealtime is a place to relax, reconnect, and get everyone together.[14]

Several studies back up Fishel's claim. These include those done by the National Center on Addiction and Substance Abuse (NCASA) at Columbia University[15] and the National Journal of Pediatrics and Child Health[16] which show family dinner time is proven to lower depression and addiction and at the same time increases self-esteem. In addition the NCASA surveyed over 1,000 teens and discovered over 84% of them prefer dinner times with family as opposed to alone. This same survey discovered that teens who eat with their parents are more likely to experience less stress and have a better relationship with their parents.[17]

When our kids reached the point where we could sit around the table together, John and I realized we had different views on the importance of family mealtime. He grew up having a meal with his family at six o'clock every evening. Short of death, near death, or a natural disaster, if you lived at home, you were expected at family dinners. This tradition continued long after all the children had left home, up until the passing of John's dad a few years ago. Dinner was on the table and you sat together. The phone did not get answered, the television stayed off, and even allowing the radio to play was a big deal. This is what you did. You sat, connected, and talked.

My upbringing was different. I recall our family sitting around the dinner table when I was younger, but as I hit the teen years, this changed. I was the biggest overachiever possible. I often came home late in the evening or stopped by for a quick bite and headed out again for a practice or work. Our family ate the same meal but at different times. Even when we were together, we usually just sat in front of the television watching a favorite show. We were near each other, but it wasn't the time to talk.

Now, don't get me wrong. My parents wanted to find out about my day, hear my thoughts, and connect—it just didn't happen at mealtime. My husband fought to get us around the table in the same manner as in his upbringing, since it was his favorite time of the day. Since our family dinnertime faded away during my teen years and never happened when I came home as an adult, I saw it as a nice but unnecessary tradition. When our kids were toddlers and we were fighting spills and tantrums, I would look at John and say, "Why are we doing this?"

But as they grew, I began to see why. The dinner table became the place we relaxed and spent time together. Our only agenda was to eat and be close. Sometimes, it was the place we would try to have family devotionals or God-times. However, I started to see it was also the easiest place to be consistent or have an important whole-family conversation because we were going to be there anyway. Yet as the kids started to squeeze into extracurricular activities, this dinnertime ritual got more difficult and complicated. We tried different mealtimes and connecting points, but Caleb came to us one day and said, "I miss dinnertime together." We realized the dinner table had become a place to find out about what was going on at school or with friends, have goofy conversations about their interests, and focus on particular topics. We have come to grips with the reality that family dinnertime may not happen every night, but it does happen several times a week. Intentionality has been the key.

When we come to the dinner table, I have a plan. Our whole family is together, and we can talk about life for a moment of time. Now some of you are saying, "Whew, we got this right. I have a plan." And others think, "I don't know when we can get a meal together next. Dad (or Mom) works late. The kids have sports, and we have little ones at home. I guess we can all wait to eat until 7:30 when all activities finish."

If you have a five year old and a fourteen year old in the same home, chances are you can't eat dinner so late. But remember, the meal is only a means to an end: creating a consistent time when your family can sit and be together. Families need all sorts of time to connect, communicate, and interact. We may not have long spans of time, but if we are focused and authentic, each moment creates another building block toward open dialogue.

· Look Who's Talking ·

I've noticed almost every website that focuses on communication with teens says parents don't know how to talk to their kids. They then go on to give their suggestions of topics to open the door. Yes, the rules have changed, and some days we're tripping forward, each blurting out a foreign language that neither can quite comprehend. However, contrary to the belief of virtually every sitcom plot line, parents are not idiots who have no idea that our kids are more than just barely alive. That might make for a good laugh, but more often than not, our antics occur because we're trying too hard, not because we're not trying at all. This is why we must grab hold of the spaces available for communication and use them to our advantage. We say, "I don't know how to talk to my kids anymore" when what we mean is, "I don't like the way it feels when they won't talk to me the way I want to."

This morning I woke up to Caleb's voice. He was chatting away with his sister in the hallway outside my bedroom. He has been sick for the last few days, so I told John, "I guess Caleb's feeling better."

He laughed and said, "Yeah, fifth-grade Caleb's awake today."

I knew exactly what he meant. Caleb has always been our most relational kid, and from about fourth through seventh grades, he would wake up and want to talk with us right away. He knew better than to try to engage his non-morning-person mother, so he would grab John's attention and talk to him about *everything*. Without taking a breath, he shared everything from his thoughts on sports to discussions on why Lucifer would want to be God. He followed John around the house talking and talking and talking all the way up until the time he left for school. One day, John walked up to the top of our stairs, turned around, and walked back down to see if Caleb would notice. He didn't. He just followed his dad and kept talking.

Sometime last year, this morning conversation slowed as hormones kicked in and he woke up a little more tired. He didn't shut down, but he engaged less. But this morning, the old Caleb emerged.

Here's the difference, though. Today, I knew we were seeing nervous Caleb. He has PSATs at school today, and they have him stressed out. Figuring out this kind of information behind the information can be tough, but getting to know our kids more and more helps. We have some routines in place in the morning that allows Caleb the space to talk and let down when he needs to. He knows his sister will be in the bathroom blow-drying her hair just as he's getting dressed. His job in the morning (by default because he has two teen sisters who take longer to get ready) is to make sure lunches are packed and all his football gear is ready to go. He also knows John will be in the kitchen puttering and making sure everyone is staying on track. Having this constant gave him the space to get out his nervous energy this morning. Sure, it would be easier to ask him to stop talking (so many words at 6:30 a.m.), and it would be easy for him to stew over his fears. Instead, the constants allowed space for everything he needed.

· Time for a Change ·

Chances are you have a few small rituals in place that you can flip and use to your benefit. If not, let's work together to create them. Think through your day with your children. What's already in place? What slight adjustments could you make to take back a few moments here and there?

A friend of mine started getting up with her high school kids to get them on the bus. She found the few minutes before they went out the door to just say, "Be amazing today" made a huge difference in her kids' lives. Sometimes, the long conversations intimidate our kids. But when you use routine to your advantage, you feel like you have more time, not less.

We also need one-on-one time with our children, and unless you have an only child, this can be a challenge. In fact, one of my close friends has an only child, and she feels like finding one-on-one time is hard, too. Since his dad travels a lot for work, she sometimes feels she and her teen son have too much time together. But she also wonders if they engage much during those times. She can also feel like whenever she wants to talk about something, her son rolls his eyes.

When she and I talked about this, I asked, "So what's a natural time of connecting with your son during the day?" "Bedtime," she said.

· Reclaiming Bedtime ·

There was probably a time when you tucked your children into bed, read them a story, and maybe even said evening prayers. We did. But as our children grew older and had more Advanced Placement classes, lessons, work, and other activities, their bedtimes got later and later. I realized I was letting them put themselves to bed and didn't even know when they went to sleep. I wasn't sure what to do. John and I decided to take bedtime back in two ways—one our kids love and one they hate. Unless they have a special project due the next day or a favorite television show to watch, our kids are headed to their rooms by 9:30 p.m. In taking this step, we realized a few things. Our kids had no need to watch television just for the sake of watching television or be on a phone or device to watch one more YouTube video. They needed time to decompress before going to sleep.

My children will tell you they hate this rule in theory because "No one else in high school still has a bedtime." But we'd noticed an unhealthy pattern in which they didn't fall asleep well because they had no real time to disconnect from the day.

At bedtime, our kids don't have to go to sleep. They just have to be in their rooms. Technology is docked and turned off. "You don't have to tell your friends you have a bedtime," we tell them. "But except for emergencies, there will be no phone calls or texts past this time." They can read, work through devotionals, finish home-work, or look over the information for that test one final time. It takes about thirty minutes to wash faces, brush teeth, and remem-ber everything they need for the next day. One evening, Kaleigh told us, "As much as I hate to admit it, I need this time to settle in for the night."

I want to reiterate: there are times when this gets pushed back. We watch a television show as a family that ends at ten. Youth group gets them home and in their rooms closer to 10:30, and weekends and vacations are a little laxer. However, in a technologi-cal, over-connected world, we've come to see the value in the lesson of shutting off.

Here's the second part to our bedtime routine: John and I visit each child separately to talk and pray. I stopped waiting until they were asleep (although unless homework is still in process, we ensure lights are off by eleven on school nights). Instead, when everyone is in their room and settled, we divide and conquer. It's funny how they don't like it when we come to their rooms together. Caleb will yell, *"No!"* when we enter at the same time. He has come to not only enjoy but look forward to his one-on-one time with each parent.

I realize your children may not all have their own rooms, or one of you may work evenings, but you can still take this concept to heart. We've changed it up when I'm traveling, when they've shared rooms, or when one of us works late. The point is to reclaim this moment that happens anyway: our kids going to their rooms and going to sleep for the night.

These small spaces of daily rituals have become the times when we most often focus on the tough topics. Our kids use these moments to discuss struggles, fears, hurts, or doubts. A few years ago, my youngest was going through a tough time with a friend—some junior high drama that broke her heart. She would hold it together until bedtime, when I would lie next to her, stroke her hair, and hold her close. We would pray about it, talk it out, and come up with a plan for interacting with the girl the next day.

Our kids use bedtime to ask about changing bodies, raging hormones, the Bible, and everything in between. We've also found that taking these times back has made it less intimidating to bring up topics we need to address. Wouldn't it be wonderful if discussions about sex, drugs, addiction, porn, and all the difficult issues could happen in one moment and be done? Sure, we may set up a focused discussion on any of these topics, but in order to help our kids navigate the world we live in, these conversations should be ongoing.

As we pay attention to our kids' love languages and personalities, we can pick up on comments they make and enter into conversations with purpose. I find it less stressful to know we'll continue the discussion than to feel like one conversation must contain all the essential elements of the birds and bees or any of the other subjects that make us stutter and blush. We discuss spiritual topics like keeping their faith, but we also share truths they need to learn about navigating relationships. Just like our times in the car, knowing the conversation has a definite endpoint makes bedtime talk safer for parent and teen.

It's also the perfect time to remind our kids that tomorrow is a new day where they can start over. At times, I've apologized when I have lectured a little too heartily or have not handled my frustration or anger well. It's the opportunity to let them know they can have a new perspective, refocus for school, or just plain get a do-over.

· Pathways for Communication ·

Saturdays are always family days at our house, and Friday night is pizza and a movie night. It's so easy to move in a million different directions and then collapse into downtimes. Yet, as much as we need to say things to our kids, sometimes we just need to have fun and spend time together. We watch, we talk, and we laugh. On at least one weekend day, we go out and do something for a few hours as a family. Yes, there are projects, friends to see, and now our kids are working, as well. But getting out and doing something fun reminds everyone that life doesn't always have to be intense. Like family dinnertimes, these relaxed moments provide open doors for the kids to be silly.

I'm thankful that John and I are blessed to complement each other in our communication style. I can have a topic ready to discuss at a drop of the hat. But he reminds me that sometimes a hike, bike ride, day at the beach, or even vacation can be taken at face value. Purposeful conversations and time together both open pathways for communication. This way we don't set up awkward moments in which we force ourselves to talk at our kids. Instead, we can truly have a back-and-forth conversation.

One ritual that hasn't worked for us is family devotional time. I didn't want to tell you, but I'd be remiss if I didn't. Of course we consider instilling a lifelong love of Christ essential—it's absolutely at the forefront every time we interact with our kids. Directly or indirectly, we tie many of our moments around the dinner table, before bed, or on the way to school to what it means to be a disciple of Jesus.

When our kids were young, John and I had a dream of opening the Bible as a family, having a lesson, and maybe doing a craft or game to bring the point home. This would one day evolve into joyous occasions of deep discussion. But it has never, ever happened this way. More accurately, when we try family devotions, one child flops, another sighs, and we end up discouraged that no one's paying attention.

We've tried different iterations such as letting the kids run the devotionals or having five-minute sessions after dinner. Currently, we've instituted Sunday evening family prayer. Creating a habit is hard, especially when it isn't already a natural part of the day. Our best option has been tying devotions to meals, because we're already there. Sometimes, we have family meetings in which we discuss a decision that needs to be made or clarify information our kids need to know. Last year, we did a pretty good job of doing an easy Advent family time I had created. But we don't have a regular pattern with any of these.

The point here is that we try and fail, but we do get our kids talking about the Lord and the Bible. Far better than a devotional, in fact, has been taking to heart the idea of talking to our kids about the Lord everywhere, all the time. This is where we take advantage of consistency. In the car after church, we always talk about the one takeaway point each person got from the sermon. At bedtime, we encourage our kids to be in the Word daily as we show them we are, too. You see, following Jesus isn't an event as much as it a lifestyle. Does that mean we stop trying to gather together to study and discuss? No, but we have come to embrace that in this area, we may just have to keep trying. And we should never be afraid to create some new traditions along the way.

We also have to remember we're merely stealing back moments already available to us. As our kids remember we're here for them, they'll want us to engage them. In this way, we're creating not only time together, but a legacy. As we use our daily schedules to our advantage, our children will learn to do the same. They might not approach it the same way, but they'll remember the spaces in their lives were filled with connection and love.

1. What are the daily rituals and routines in your family's life?

2. Pick two of these and write out ideas for how you could better use those to connect with your kids.

3. Name something you might like to talk to your kids about at bedtime tonight.

4. Describe the legacy of connection you would like to create in your home.

···One Bite for Today···

Remember that connecting with your kids is more important than the specific topic of conversation. Pick one daily routine today and use it to listen to your children and learn a little bit more about who they really are.

Chapter 6

School Projects:
Life Lessons on Poster Board

'm staring at my kitchen table littered with scraps of clay, feathers, and sand. Yes, sand. You can't imagine how much I love having the corners of every room in my house filled with stray markers and strips of ribbon.

I know. You're thinking I must homeschool or have young children and you missed it thus far. Nope. I'm reflecting on the current state of my home with three teens who go to school every day. We're in the midst of two science fair projects and a history fair project. Do my words make sense now?

· School Daze ·

This probably isn't the chapter you were expecting in a book about navigating adolescence. If you homeschool, I have the greatest respect for you, because you're in charge of every aspect of your children's learning. But no matter what the school setting, I think it's easy for parents to just have a "Git 'Er Done" attitude about school. As long as we make sure they finish their homework, study for tests, and aren't struggling, all is well. But John and I have come to see school as anything but simple.

Think about it. When was the last time a school project ate up your weekend (and, let's face it, your wallet)? That's right, you, the parent. Remember when that non-art teacher decided to get creative? You had other plans that may have involved something *you* found fun. Instead, you were relegated indoors where your dining room table may or may not have survived. You searched the house for a shoebox. You wandered up and down the aisles of Michael's or Hobby Lobby or even Home Depot while your child searched for the perfect Styrofoam, paint, stickers, and poster board swag. You left feeling like you were about to buy an A for $50 or less.

Not long ago, I was purchasing some supplies with my daughter when the dad behind us in line tapped me on the shoulder and asked, "Why don't we just give the school direct access to our bank accounts? It would be more effective."

I used to think this era of projects would end as research papers grew more frequent. I never dreamed my child's eighth-grade teacher would say to me, "I expect parents to help with this project. This isn't just for them; it's for you. Use this to bring your family together."

Three months later after building a miniature replica of the New Jersey boardwalk, endless sessions of encouraging our son to be proactive, and hours upon hours of work, John walked up to the same teacher on the due date. "This did not bring us closer," he declared with a grin—and walked away.

· Do It Yourself ·

It may not have brought us closer, but it did remind us of life lessons that can come through glue and paint. You see, we're the parents who actually require our children to do projects themselves. Our job is to be there for moral support and in case of a breakdown. Yes, my child was the fifth-grader who spent twelve hours recreating a scene from *Percy Jackson, Lightning Thief* out of clay only to discover a classmate, who, with obvious help, built a full-scale version of Bilbo Baggins' house from *The Hobbit*. A child who had done this alone should have been sent to an institute for gifted artists. But this kid didn't, and he wasn't.

Our policy means our kids' projects are not always perfect, and the perfectionist in me goes a little crazy when the borders tilt or the poster board's too busy. Yet there's power in teaching our kids to take ownership of their own work. This isn't about whether or not the child is a good student, feels smart, or even likes school projects. Instead, it's about looking to the future and the goal to release our children into adulthood well.

Recently, John and I were talking about our own school memories of high school projects. John recalls an argument that ended with his dad yelling, "Fine, do it yourself," and John responding, "Fine, I will."

John got an A. After that, when it came to projects, he was left to sink or swim on his own .

My parents were more hands-on (truthfully too hands on at times), but they used the years of helping me with projects to instill a work ethic about pushing ahead, creativity, and doing my best. I, too, came to that moment where I declared, "Hey, could I do this on my own?" My parents were glad to let that happen but waited for the times I needed help. (This usually involved my dad staying up until the wee hours of the morning to finish typing a paper I had put off until the last minute.)

As our kids moved past elementary school, our varied experiences caused John and me to approach the project arena differently. We realized those elementary-school dioramas were great catalysts for learning. There came a point, though, when John felt like our kids should go out on their own, and I thought we should wait in the shadows to swoop in as needed. We had to agree that each of us learned lessons, good and bad, from our parents' responses. He learned to work harder, and I learned how to ask for help when I was struggling.

Unintentionally, this also reinforced my tendency to procrastinate. I was involved in everything and, if I applied myself, could get excellent grades. I could also use my wits to mismanage time and still be in the top ten percent of my class. John, on the other hand, didn't always ask for help when he needed it. If he couldn't figure things out himself, his attitude was, "It's good enough."

Everything we learned worked itself out one way or another in college, and we straightened out. Despite their different approaches, both sets of our parents used school projects to teach some lessons that would set us up well for the rest of our lives: Work hard, as hard as you can. Do your best in everything put before you.

School projects are an opportunity for our kids to learn how to order their work, manage time, solve problems, and follow leadership. No matter how much a child struggles with a subject, the project gives them a chance to shine. These are just a few of the lessons we all learned as students, and they're important for our kids to learn as well.

· Proactive Plus ·

Proactive is the most powerful word my children have learned when it comes to their schoolwork (and life in general). Perhaps it's an overreaction to my own ability to procrastinate or what I like to call "work well under pressure." It could also be that my children can stare at technology for hours on end and then somehow make it my fault that they didn't get to their homework. "I told you I needed help," is the common excuse.

"Well, what could you have done while you were waiting?"

(Blank stare.)

It could also be that one of my kids has a ridiculously keen sense of time management. It is not uncommon for me to find said child in their room working on homework over a school vacation. When we ask, "What are you doing?" they map out the next three weeks and how it's best if they can get ahead—all while their clothes have taken over the floor of their room. Learning to be proactive will help even the most studious kid succeed.

Here's the truth as we've learned it via our children: The artistic ones don't care about the actual information that has to go into the project. They just want to make it look awesome. The procrastinating ones told us about the project that's due tomorrow at seven o'clock the night before. The perfectionist ones cry because they can't make it look the way it does in their mind's eye. However, learning to think a few steps ahead will help each of them come to the end with a project they're proud to turn in.

To help your child learn to be proactive, ask them to map out all of the elements of the project. When is it due? How much research will it require? Could they make a supply list or at least share what their grand idea for constructing the Roman Coliseum out of toothpicks will entail? The first step in every project that comes through the door is proactivity.

· Lifetime Learning ·

Even as they get older, it would still be easy to jump in and just do projects for our kids. Last year, Kaleigh decided to cut out more than seven hundred squares of tissue paper to create a realistic bush for her biology project. No, it wasn't the way I would have done it, but the final project was amazing. This is one of the hardest lessons for us parents to learn. If our child has worked with excellence and diligence and followed directions, they've done a wonderful job.

Projects help our kids get excited about learning for a lifetime. It's easy for some kids to do little more than endure school. In my own home I have one who loves the traditional style of sharing information, research, and notes; another who loves experiments and hands-on activities; and still another who loves being creative. Projects provide great opportunities to explore something new in a style that fits each child. The end result affirms them as learners both now and in the future.

· Mountains to Climb ·

Have you seen your kids compare themselves to others and say, "They're smarter than I am?" I think at some point, every parent wishes their children could skip past the school years and into adulthood. Once you get that diploma, no one knows whether you got an A in Math or happen to be better in Art than Chemistry. Instead, we take the skills we've learned and apply them.

Our children need to know that being intelligent doesn't always coincide with grades achieved or a particular class ranking. As a wise-beyond-his-years Christopher Robin reminded his friend Winnie the Pooh, "Promise me you'll always remember: You're braver than you believe, stronger than you seem, and smarter than you think."[18] Our kids need to take the power of these words to heart now, before they leave home. Otherwise, they'll stop in their tracks when they meet a new challenge. They'll stare, frozen in fear, at the hurdle in front of them, figuring out how to avoid rather than conquer it.

Don't we all want our kids to come to the foot of a mountain and figure out the best way to climb it? Sure, they can always go around. The terrain on the climb is too rough, they feel inadequate for the ascent, and it will be beyond difficult to reach the summit. But if they choose the easy way, they'll miss the view at the top, remaining stuck in the valley with a different set of challenges. Let's teach our kids to take the mountain head-on.

It may seem like a far reach, but these school projects set the stage for our kids to learn how to work through difficulty and not give up. One day, a blood-curdling scream came from our dining room (what I like to call Project Headquarters). "What, what?" I asked, sprinting into the room.

"It's ruined."

"What are you talking about?" My child didn't appear hurt, and the project looked fine.

"I can't fit the title across the top of the board, and now I have to start all over."

"Umm, let's think this through."

We discussed a few options she didn't like and finally came up with a plan. I then put my mad skills (acquired through many a messed-up project back in the day) to work. We carefully razor-bladed the sticker letters off the board, realigned them, and covered the one ripped corner with a strategically placed picture. My child had unintentionally learned how to tackle a problem in a variety of ways and be tenacious in working toward a solution.

· Group Effort ·

Team projects can teach valuable lessons, which is, of course, why teachers assign them. John and I consider these the worst of the worst in project-land. The group always ends up at our house, so we end up putting out all the money on supplies. And somehow, these group projects always happen at the most inconvenient times. Yes, parents, we hate group projects. Yet I've watched them help my kids blossom into people who can navigate working with others in ways they need to remember.

Just a month ago, a student approached Bethany and asked if she could be her partner in an upcoming assignment for history class. This girl wanted my daughter as a partner because she knew Bethany would work hard for an A, and my daughter realized this.

She could have turned the other girl away or brooded over the pairing. Instead, she told her, "I'd love to work with you, but we're going to both put in equal work and do our best." The other girl responded, "Yes, I guess I could put in enough effort for a B."

Again, instead of getting frustrated, Bethany said, "No, let's both work our best and aim for an A. We can figure this out together." This inspired her partner that not only could Bethany do well, but she could as well. And they turned out to be the perfect duo. My daughter made sure the grammar, research, and editing were perfect, and the other girl put her creativity to work and gave the project some outstanding details.

On the other hand, Kaleigh's recent project has made me want to pull out all my hair. Between the lack of initial information from the teacher and the requirement that the kids work on the project after school hours, I've screamed into a pillow every day since it came home. Still, like her sister's, this project has provided a great opportunity to walk Kaleigh through problem-solving and people skills.

· Don't Back Off ·

So much of our kids' time is spent in school, and as parents, we can't afford not to take an interest in their grades and futures. We must stop holding their hands and allow them to take steps in the process of becoming lifelong learners. This is why don't get to back off completely. Let's remind them they can always learn more and go farther. We never know it all.

Beauty in ACTION

1. When was the last time your child had to do a school project, and how did it affect your family?

2. How might you help your children learn to be proactive with their next school project?

3. Thinking of the last school project your child did, what was the biggest lesson they learned?

4. How can we instill a love of learning in our children?

···One Bite for Today···

Have you heard rumors about an upcoming school project? What is one life lesson you would like your child to learn in the midst of it? Help them focus and remind them that you notice when they give their best.

Chapter 7

Butting Heads: When Everything Feels Like a Standoff

Once upon a time, a certain young woman had the bad habit of never cleaning her room. Always littered with clothes, it was rarely picked up or presentable. Her mother asked, even begged her to put her clothes in the dressers provided for storage. But this teen liked her "pile" system.

One afternoon, she called home after school to tell her mom band practice would run late. "OK," her mom said. "Just to let you know, I've given my last lecture about your room. So today, I got everything off the floor, loaded it into trash bags, and took them to the dump."

"What?! My clothes? All my stuff?"

Livid only began to describe the girl's feelings as fire coursed through her veins and the tears ran just as hot. Didn't Mom know everything down there was special? Besides, everybody knows your favorite clothes are the ones that hit the floor most often.

That day, I changed my approach to cleaning my room.

Yes, I was the teen with the infamous pile system. Months later, on Christmas morning, you can imagine my surprise when I unwrapped a large box containing all my favorites from Mom's day of floor-purging. She never had to take such a drastic step again—but that wasn't the last time we butted heads.

· Game On—or Not ·

Maintaining order and obedience in the home is something parents start figuring out once their children learn to be their own people, which is pretty much as soon as they leave the womb. On a recent flight to Chicago, I had the pure joy of sitting behind a couple with a baby. At one point I looked up from my book to find the baby's wide eyes peering at me from over the top of his pacifier. We stared at each other for a long while without blinking, so I did what any respectable mother does when she encounters a baby: I began a rousing game of peek-a-boo. As this continued, his mom leaned in to her now-giggling baby and asked, "Can I have a kiss?"

With a huge, emphatic shake of his head, this little cutie refused her affection. Her eyes went wide and the game was on. "Can I have a kiss?" she would ask, and he would turn his head away. (She, of course, would follow through with a huge kiss on the cheek.)

When our children are babies, the answer *no* is adorable. When they don't want to give us a kiss we giggle, and we see each set of defiance as a new opportunity to teach them right from wrong. Then around the toddler years when they start to answer "no" to all requests the "cute" wears off. Before we know it we are standing toe to toe with a person barely as tall as our knee, exhausted with tantrums and fits, as we try to show them we are here to keep them safe and bring direction.

By the time our kids reach adolescence, we think we've figured some things out. We made it past the biting phase, and then the elementary school ages sort of made sense. At this point, we know they can understand our guidance and expectations are clear. Then all of a sudden, a shift happens, and our children seem to become more defiant, apathetic, or both. They tell us, "All you do is lecture me" and sigh as they walk way.

These moments have convinced me that my children must have a teenage version of dementia. I didn't know it was possible to "forget" how to empty the dishwasher or remember the floor of your room is not the appropriate place to put your clothes away. I recently made the discovery that asking your teenage son to shower after a four-hour athletic practice that involves a helmet, layers of padding, and running in ninety-seven-degree weather with eighty percent humidity is a crime against humanity. Apparently, he didn't notice that the stench was so overpowering that we drove home with air conditioning blasting and all of the windows down.

· Control Freak? ·

John and I have amazing children who, I truly believe, long to follow the Lord. But that doesn't mean they don't occasionally make poor choices, and it definitely doesn't mean we always handle those situations well. So if you're looking for the perfect formula to raise perfect children, you may want to go ahead and skip this chapter. Also, keep in mind that some things you already do in your family work well. This is not a charge to throw out the old and start something new. Instead, use the ideas given here alongside what you're doing now.

When Bethany was a baby. I read a devotional that forever changed our approach to parenting and especially this idea of order in the home. The one-page charge reminded us that our role is not to be in control of the lives of our children. We aren't responsible for manipulating their behavior. Our job does not include building their lives for them. Instead, our responsibility is to teach our children how to read the blueprint God has drawn out for them with Him as foundation.

You see, we can't "make" our children do anything. A person can lead a horse to water, stick their head in the water, shove water in the horse's mouth, and massage it down their throat, but not make them enjoy the refreshment of a drink. However, we can show the horse the benefits of the water, teach them how to drink the water, and make sure they know how to find more water in the future. And that's the approach we need to take with our kids. As we face the challenges of guiding them through the various ages, we can fall into the trap of simply wanting to dominate our kids and make them do what they should.

· The Toughest Job We'll Ever Love ·

Over the years of parenting, my husband and I have learned that discipline is much more about reaching our children's hearts rather than setting up rules. Yes, there are principles we can follow, but we have to figure out what works best for our own children with their own personalities in our own family. Our ultimate goal is not for them to learn to "act right." Instead, we want their worldview to be transformed into an understanding of true life with Christ. God is clear on wanting our whole lives, not just our hearts.

Yes, Christ wants authority over our lives, and the cost is our entire selves, including our obedience. God does not want us to merely go through the motions but to follow Him closely. For this reason, He did not set up a series of rules for us to follow as much as a boundary system to keep us safe. If He had been looking for a bunch of rule-followers, Jesus wouldn't have had so many strong words to the Pharisees, whom He called "whitewashed tombs" (Matt. 23:27). In other words, "You like to stick a fresh coat of paint on death and call it good."

The religious leaders were great at following rules, but they totally missed their Messiah. This is why we can't focus on behavior modification with our kids, although that's often what we'd prefer. It's easier to say "Don't" and "Stop" than to focus on transforming their worldview one step at a time. However, if we are truly looking to the people we hope them to become, and our end game is a vibrant follower of Christ who also happens to be a responsible adult, we must look beyond today.

This long-term perspective also means we can't throw up our hands and declare, "Oh well, I guess this is who they are now." If that's the case, my children have missed some valuable life lessons, and there's nothing I can do. Instead, we dig in our heels for the toughest job we'll ever love. We focus on helping our children grab hold of a worldview that helps them understand how to live for Christ. Yes, sometimes we want to scream when, because of their extreme attachment to a mobile device, they "forget" to do the chore we asked them to do five hours ago. Each of us has fallen into bed on at least one occasion wondering, "Will my child ever get it together?"

Sure, we could limp through these years and just wait for them to move out. But who wants that kind of misery? So embrace the long look at parenting—and as I've mentioned before, hold on for the ride of your life.

· Boundary Lines ·

Like building a fence around a backyard, putting boundaries in place has helped our family create consistency and clarity in our expectations. When Bethany first got a cell phone, we made the "rule" that at any time and in any area (calls, texts, social media) we could check her history. And we do. We also started using the word *accountability* to explain expectations like this to our kids. As Bethany began to push back on the edges of our family fence, it was as though she kept asking, "Don't you trust me to wander outside that gate? I can handle life out there."

But the issue isn't whether our kids can deal with it or handle life on the outside of our home. Jesus wants us on the narrow path matching His stride because only that will bring us the fullest life. The Lord didn't give us the Ten Commandments or the various New Testament guidelines because He's a cosmic killjoy but because of His everlasting love. It isn't that He doesn't trust us. He wants what's best for us. The moment we start to believe He's holding out, we lose.

This is the bigger concept we want to share with our kids. It's also why we started letting them know we hold them accountable to live fully, safely, and in Christ. We, as their parents, hold them accountable for now. As they move forward to the day they leave home, they'll need a variety of accountability partners, beyond merely their parents to check their boundaries. This is all a part of learning to walk with Jesus forever.

Of course, this doesn't mean my children never complain about their guidelines and boundaries. I haven't raised cherubs who spout, "Yes, Mother, I will immediately do everything you ask." Sometimes, their attitudes and actions can result in deep anger that leads to yelling or the dreaded parental lecture. John often says to our kids, "There is something you can do about all of these constant reminders we give you" (code for what they consider a lecture). "You can actually follow through on what we ask."

· Strategies for Success ·

Every parenting book in the universe will tell you the importance of consistency. When our kids get to a certain age, though, parents believe they should be able to figure out what they're supposed to do. It can boggle our minds when they defiantly choose to ignore our requests, and when we call them out on it, they tell us, "I forgot." Seriously? The curfew for technology has been in place for a year. You can't remember it's nine o'clock tonight and every night?

The way to remain consistent is to remain clear on our expectations. We map out the consequences to missing the mark and then we follow through. If we realize we created confusion about an expectation, our kids get one pass. The next time they "forget," they know what will happen, and we follow through. We even ask questions like "What's the consequence if you forget to turn off your phone/iPod at 9:00 p.m.?" They answer, "I lose it for twenty-four hours." The boundary is clear.

Boundaries create clarity about expectations, yet each of our children is unique and pushes on the edges of the fence in different ways. Some children scream and rant when they disagree with our parenting decisions, others debate (they're right and Mom and Dad are wrong, of course), and still others quietly stand their ground, brooding. This means we must have consistent expectations with an individualized approach.

Since our kids were small, we've avoided ambiguous statements like "Be good." Who knows what that means? And of course, every child defines *good* differently. In other words, just because your disobedience is quiet doesn't make it any less defiant. I've also learned not to toss out statements like "Why can't you be more (or less) . . ." These comments help no one.

Watching how each of our children reacts differently has made John and me rethink how we respond when they disobey. Lecturing may make us feel better, but it rarely changes anyone or anything. So we modified the way we deal with our children when they try to run from safety. It also means John and I have to take turns when our kids get out of control. Making statements like "Wait until your mother/father gets home" only strips a parent of respect.

But we must also recognize the words and actions from our kids that may make us angry and keep us from responsible interaction. Sometimes triggers that have little to do with our kids set us off: eye rolling, a sarcastic "Whatever," or stomping up the stairs. We need to identify which issues are ours and which come from our kids. Their behavior may be wrong, but without care and wisdom, our responses can be wrong as well.

Sometimes, with a defiant child, it helps to tag out and wait a second, take a breath, and reengage. We often use this moment to hug the child and remind them we love them, even in the midst of what seems to be a battle. Remember, there are at least two pieces in play in this scenario: the behavior and the heart issue behind it. A hug and an apology for any anger on your part helps change their perspective and can ultimately help transform their worldview.

At this point, we remind the child of the boundaries we have in place that apply to this situation. Again, accountability allows them to know exactly what our expectations are.

· Get Creative ·

Overarching boundaries, however, don't always work with ongoing issues (remember my teenage preference for the pile system?). In these cases, you may need to follow my mom's example and find a creative approach—although I don't advocate lying to your kids. I admit that John and I tried some fresh ideas out of desperation. No matter how consistent we were, we couldn't get our kids to listen about certain things, and the same heart-issues kept arising.

Our family faced this in the issue of sibling rivalry. Two of our children couldn't seem to understand how to get along with each other. So we got creative. We renamed a small loveseat in our living room the "Kindness Couch" and set a boundary that said they had to sit next each other for two minutes for every minute of fighting. We don't allow technology on the Kindness Couch, so they can't ignore each other. Couch sessions usually start with complaining and end with laughter.

Another method has been the idea of "serving the one who

makes you angry." If fighting gets out of control, we ask both parties (or sometimes all three) to swap chores with their siblings or to serve them in some other way. They might have to clean each other's rooms or make each other's lunches. The key element of this strategy is that both have to participate in the same task. The first time two of my kids had to make each other's lunches, each was afraid the other would spit on their sandwich. Serving one another forces a shift in perspective. And we don't require it, but we strongly suggest that they pray for their sibling while serving them.

Finally, we've tried an "exchange of words" approach in which they must exchange every negative word spoken about their sibling for something positive. "She's stupid" requires "My sister's really smart." This helps kids learn how to consider what they love about people, not what makes them angry.

So yes, create a boundary system for your home that creates clear guidelines for expectations across the board. Then prepare to try some ideas that might work with each child. The expectations are the same, but the consequences are different for each of our kids. One might lose phone privileges while another will miss an activity or event. My friends and I actually compare notes of creative approaches like the Great Clothes Toss of '87. My goal, again, is not to give you a formula. You need to assess your home, your family, and what's important to you for your children.

If you have kids who are out of control, there are experts out there who are far more qualified than I am at helping you navigate those waters. That is not really the focus of this chapter. We have included some ideas for resources in the endnotes of the book. My kids are hard workers, seek to love and be loved by the Lord, and want to be respectful at home. But they're still growing and maturing. They need accountability, boundaries, and to learn how to look at the world through the eyes of obedience to Christ. That's why this book emphasizes communication. Keeping the communication lines open between you and your child smooths out many difficult situations.

· Coaching and Caring ·

The final piece to a great home discipline system is what I call "coaching." This is different than a lecture, tirade, or dissertation about how our kids should act. Coaching says to them, "I love you. These are the consequences to what just happened. Next time, you'll handle it better." Coaching is coming back into your child's room after a confrontation ends and reminding them of who they are in the Lord. Look them in the eye and say, "We're not done with you yet, and God will never give up on you."

Coaching also helps us assess the moments when our children need some grace because they messed up and they know it. Remember, you're working toward an understanding of repentance and a genuine heart change. Let them know why you love them and that one misstep doesn't make a bad person. Remind them of the expectations and, if you need to follow through on a consequence, do so.

We handle coaching with what we like to call the "sandwich." Begin with a compliment, a truth about who your child is. This might be something like "You have a personality that desires to lead people." The middle of the sandwich contains the coaching moment or "next time" statement. "Sometimes in your desire to lead, you can sound bossy or your words can hurt others' feelings. Let's think through some ways to approach your brother with different words or tone next time." Then finish your sandwich with a compliment: "I see that your heart is to be a leader and to see people move in the right direction. I love that God gave you such an awesome quality."

Think about the standard version of that scenario: "You were bossing your brother around, and you need to stop. It creates a fight every time." Instead, we can coach them through it by placing direction between encouragement. In this insecurity-laden season of their life, they don't need to hear "You're bad." A wise coach will say, "Let's continue to grow together."

The key to order in all our homes is a vibrant, lifelong relationship with our Lord for parent and child. Let's remember to help them walk this out.[19]

Beauty in ACTION

1. List three things you wish your children could remember to do the first time you ask them? (We like to say, "All the way, right away, with a happy heart.")

   a.

   b.

   c.

2. Brainstorm some boundaries for your family in the following areas:

   a. Chores:

   b. Technology:

   c. Behavior:

3. Return to the list above and write down these three details for each item:

   a. *Clear Expectation.* (Technology is turned off at 9 p.m.)

b. *Consequence for Ignoring the Expectation.* (Lose technology use for 24 hours.)

c. *Ability to follow through.* (Lose all technology or may use phone only for calling after sports practice. Follow-up consequence if found disobeying again.)

4. Think of a recent confrontation with one or more of your children. What's one "next time" statement you could have made? Try to find a time when you can apply this coaching technique.

5. Write down something for which you need to apologize to your children. Then do it.

···One Bite for Today···

I can't express enough how much you need to keep doing what you're already doing. Your kids will experience whiplash if you change everything overnight. This chapter is meant to help you shift your philosophy to keep the end in sight. Clarify, take a deep breath, and only put into action what you know you can and will follow through on. Avoid empty threats.

Chapter 8

When They Doubt:
"But I Thought Their Faith Was Strong!"

All our kids were relatively young when they came to us and said they wanted to have a personal relationship with Jesus. It made sense to them early on, and they wanted to walk out life with Him. I remember clearly that when Bethany was only four, I peppered her with questions to see if she could really comprehend sin and redemption at such a young age. Before any of my kids even went to school, they had begun to tell us how Jesus died on the cross to take away their sin and rose from the tomb to conquer death for their sake.

· The Shift ·

But when each of them hit around ten years old, something happened. My children, who were the first in their classes to memorize an entire psalm, could talk to strangers about why they needed to know Christ, and knew all their Bible stories, started to have questions about their faith. These were no longer minor quandaries with quick and easy, go-to answers from Scripture like "What are angels?" or "What do we know about Heaven?" Instead, they started asking questions like "How do I know God hears my prayers?" "Why doesn't He answer my prayers the way I'd like Him to?" "How do I really put my faith in God?" "What does that mean?" or even "If I can't see God, how can I know He is who He says He is?"

All of a sudden, hiding in the folds of their parents' faith is not enough for our kids, and they start to wrestle with what they believe. We can't just tell them what to believe anymore. They want to take hold of faith for themselves.

This questioning and confusion is called doubt. Merriam-Webster defines the word as "1. Uncertainty of belief or opinion that often interferes with decision-making; 2. A state of affairs giving rise to uncertainty, hesitation, or suspense; 3: a lack of confidence."[20] It's not necessarily about searching out other religions or truths. While our kids may have heard the facts about God every day of their lives, they want to know the "why" behind them.

I confess it often shocks me when our kids come to us with questions I think we've often discussed. They have two parents who love Christ and are in full-time ministry. They've grown up in Christian schools with a biblical worldview, they go to church often, and yet they grapple with what I see as basics.

· Faith Questions ·

Let's face it. We can't see Jesus with our eyes, touch Him with our fingertips, or text Him and get a reply. He doesn't post selfies on Instagram or write blogs so we can learn what He's up to with a simple online search. For all other subjects and people, we have constant, never-ending access. If I don't know something, I can go to a phone, iPod, tablet, or computer and look up the answer right away. So when we have questions about God and can't resolve them in less than thirty seconds, we think something must be wrong.

In this instant-gratification world, teens can unintentionally become hyper-focused on what they *do* to show their identification with Christ. They can work through a checklist of what a good person does and still have doubts. People talk about Him being close, seeing Him all around us or even feeling Him in their hearts, but that may not make sense to our kids.

Bethany had a horrible time with this. I can still remember sitting around the dinner table one night when she was about eleven and she broke down sobbing. We had asked each of our children, "What does it mean to belong to Jesus?"

Kaleigh, who was eight at the time, said, "Well, it means we are totally His. We know He died on the cross and then came back to life, and so now we are His children. It means He forgives our sins and wants us." Since Kaleigh has always been our challenging child, the idea of sin, forgiveness, and grace was easy for her to grasp. But after she shared, Bethany erupted. "I don't know the answer to that question. What's wrong with me?"

Caleb, on the other hand, went through a period when he went forward anytime someone offered to pray with him to become a follower of Christ. I think his fourth-grade teacher thought I was stone-hearted when she ran to me after school one day to tell me he had gone forward in chapel to become a believer. This was the fourth time he had done it that year alone. I smiled and thanked her.

Caleb kept wrestling with questions like "Am I saved? What does that mean? How do I know I'm going to Heaven?" No matter how many times we explained the concept of faith or tried to help him, he was convinced that just following wasn't enough. We explained that we can always get closer to the Lord, but he didn't have to keep "getting saved" every time he had a concern. We finally reached the point where we made him wait instead of going forward again and again. Yes, I've seen firsthand the ways my own children have grappled in their faith, even if the ways they expressed it were different. I wish it looked identical so I would have known exactly how to approach it. However, their hearts are the same: they want to know Jesus for themselves and not via their relationship with others who love Him.

· Doubt Happens ·

Sometimes we struggle when our kids express doubt because we may have the same questions. "Why is God silent?" "Why is life so hard?" "Where is God when I need Him most?" Such concerns may tug at the edges of our own minds. Doubts can make us feel guilty that we don't trust the Lord enough or don't cling close enough to Him. So how can we possibly help our kids?

First, we must come to the realization that doubt happens to all of us. The difference is how we deal with it. Having questions about God is part of our journey through life with Him. It's our choice if we let it lead us closer to or further away. You see, there's a difference between doubt and unbelief. Unbelief is being closed to learning more or seeking out answers to your questions. Doubt is figuring out why we believe what we do.

We can also struggle when our kids express doubt because we fear we can't deal with their questions. What if we answer them wrong? What if we end up as the reason our children never follow Jesus? It seems almost daily a new study comes out about how young people are walking away from the church and the Lord. The Pew Research Center surveyed over 35,000 adults and released their results in May of 2015. While this study showed that America still holds the highest population of Christians of any nation in the world, the number is declining. What is the greatest population of those leaving the church? Young adults.[21] CNN actually summed up the report this way: "It's not as if young people today are being raised in a way completely different from Christianity," said Smith, the Pew researcher. "But as adults they are simply dropping that part of their identity."[22] On the topic of young adults leaving their faith, Ed Stetzer of Lifeway Research has this to say, "The reason that many church-attending young adults stopped going to church upon graduating from high school is their faith just wasn't personally meaningful to them. They did not have a firsthand faith. The church had not become a valued and valuable expression in their life—one that impacts how they live and how they relate and how they grow."[23]

Teens want authenticity, to see their parents live out their own faith, and to be guided in how to grow beyond just "getting saved." They want to know how to take ownership of their faith.

Of course we want our kids to have a vibrant relationship with Christ. But sometimes, the struggle goes beyond answering hard questions. We sometimes wish our own relationship with Christ was deeper. We want our kids to understand the radical, life-shattering love of Jesus in such a way that all they can do is live for Him. But too often, we don't feel like that ourselves and wonder if we're going through the motions in our own faith.

Maturity has taught me that God's truth is not contingent on how I feel, and I'm thankful. But as our children work through the doubting process, we have to make an honest assessment of our own relationship with Jesus. Instead of reacting out of fear over our inadequacies, we need to remember that the foundation has been laid and allow the Lord to do the heavy lifting.

• Prayer Power •

Our first thought in navigating this season of doubt in our kids' lives was that there must be some experts who could answer their questions. We found some good books, but few that dealt with doubt. Lee Strobel's book *The Case for Faith for Kids* does have a chapter on this topic.[24] As we studied, we began to see some things that could help our kids.

Helping them work through their doubts starts and ends with prayer. John and I prayed for and with our kids. Prayer is so much a part of who we are as a family that I sometimes forget its power to connect us to God.

As Bethany grappled with her place with the Lord, and Caleb wondered about his heart being right, we encouraged them to talk to God. But we've learned that sometimes, we have to demystify prayer for our kids. They hear us pray (or not pray) and think there's a secret to doing it well. We often tell our children, "I think the God of the universe who made everything, including you, can handle anything you want to share with Him."

Jeremiah 29:11-13 (our family verse you may remember) says, "For I know the plans I have for you," declares the Lord, "plans to prosper you and not to harm you, plans to give you hope and a future. Then you will call on me and come and pray to me, and I will listen to you. You will seek me and find me when you seek me with all your heart." We call this a circular passage because it shows a never-ending circle of seeking and understanding that begins and ends with Him. Often, our kids comprehend God's power and holiness far more than his accessibility. When we urge them to talk to God, we know he won't play hide-and-seek. We like to tell them, "I'll pray first, and then you pray."

Our family has learned the power of being still and knowing he is God. Together, we ask Him questions and wait for answers.

But we do have to make sure our kids understand He isn't a holy vending machine who takes our request and spits out the answer we want. Instead, we're learning together to seek after Him.

· Word Power ·

Our next big revelation was that our kids had to start reading the Word for themselves every day. I can't even remember the number of Christian leaders I have heard talk about the impact of children watching their parents read their Bibles. Even recently I read an article by Todd Brady of Lifeway who mentioned, "We often teach what we know, but we reproduce who we are. Telling your child to read the Bible will fall on deaf ears if he does not see you reading it for yourself."[25] In our age of technology, though, this isn't as clear as it used to be. Once upon a time, children might see a parent with a Bible open at the breakfast table. Brady makes this true statement in the same post, "Children should see that their parents are Bible readers. When boys see their dad's Bible next to his chair and when they see him regularly reading his Bible, they grow in their understanding of the importance of Bible reading. They may rightly think, if Dad does it, it must be a big deal. When it comes to lessons children learn from their parents, more is caught than taught. The habit of reading the Bible is something your child should "catch" from you."[26] I wholeheartedly agree. However, now we have our Bibles on our phones or tablets. My children kiss me goodbye on their way to school and may think I am checking Facebook, when actually I am reading my Bible. So to "catch" Bible reading from parents involves discussing how and when we read our Bible with our children. We learned that while our children saw Scripture as important, they weren't reading it for themselves on a daily basis.

When we don't understand God's character, lies and confusion seep in. But if our kids are spending time in His Word, even on those days when they can't see the truth, they can rest in the power of who God is and what He believes about them. As Ephesians 2:10 (NLT) says, "For we are God's masterpiece. He has created us anew in Christ Jesus, so we can do the good things He planned for us long ago."

Christ changes us. He sees us as His work of art and has an important mission for us. This is just one verse in a sea of so much our kids need to take to heart. And the only way they can grasp the truth of God's Word is to make time for it every day.

I can remember sitting with Bethany and saying, "If you want to know God, you need to take the time to get to know Him." Prayer was imperative, but so was God's Word. She had to spend daily time in her Bible, not as a rule or requirement, but as a way to meet the needs of anyone who was genuinely seeking God. We made sure she had a translation that was easy to read and suggested some places to start, even if all she read was two or three verses a day.

Two years later, when Caleb started wrestling with his relationship with the Lord, we tried the same conversations and prayers we had with Bethany. But he kept circling back around to the fact he couldn't "feel" God. One night at dinner as he was talking about this, we said, "Bethany, what has helped you in your own process?" She looked at her brother and said, "You need to start reading your Bible every day. You can't trust someone you don't know. Get to know God, the real One, not the one others tell us about."

She had just repeated the mantra we used with her for two years. We don't tell our deepest darkest secrets to a stranger on the street. Why? We don't know them. We share our lives, hopes, and fears with those we know best.

Caleb started reading his Bible every day, and it has helped tremendously in his walk with the Lord. Regardless of their personality differences, we need to get our kids into the habit of having their own daily time with Jesus. They can download devotionals onto a mobile device or read books that interpret Scripture, but a chunk a day in the Bible itself is non-negotiable. We encourage our kids to write a verse on a sticky note and put it on their mirror or in a school notebook so they can reflect on it several times a day. Memorizing Scripture—not as an assignment but as part of their walk with God—is something else we recommended as they grew in their faith.

Partnering with trusted adults has been invaluable during this season in our kids' lives. We've told their youth pastors, leaders, and coaches some of the questions we're walking through so we can work together. Sometimes, our children need to hear the same truth from various people so they know it isn't just their parents' opinion. Instead of replacing our relationship with our children, these people add an extra point of view they may need to hear.

· Unanswerable ·

But every kid doesn't have the same issue of wrestling with faith. Kaleigh sees the world in absolutes: right and wrong, good or bad, truth or lies. For her, Jesus is the Savior. Why on earth would we question that? Instead, she wants answers for the gray areas of her faith.

As parents, we have to get comfortable with saying, "I don't know." There are different ways to say it, of course. Sometimes we sit down and search out the answer together. In other categories, we know the broad answer but need to affirm to our children that it's all right to hurt. "I prayed for PopPop to be well, and he died. Why didn't God hear my prayers?"

These are the times we hold our kids and let them cry. We can't answer all the questions, and I don't think God intends us to. In these cases, we point our children back to the character of God and the ways He has taken care of us in the past. For those questions we can't answer, we have to trust the Lord enough to let Him take care of it. If we keep bringing these things before Him, if the desire of our heart is to find out who He is, He won't let us down. This understanding has been invaluable in helping Kaleigh with her faith.

· Dear John ·

The story of John the Baptist in prison helps us sum up what our kids may experience during this season of doubt. Imagine you've given your whole life to loving and serving God. Not only have you given Him everything, but you've done some crazy things for Him like eating bugs and wearing weird clothes. You tell people they need to look for the Messiah, their Savior. Some think you're a lunatic, while others hear your words and recognize their truth. This is how you spend your life, laying aside everything so others might come to know Jesus— until the day you're thrown in jail for being a wacko for the Lord.

While you're imprisoned, the king of the land throws a huge party. In a moment of silliness, he allows a teenage girl to catch his eye. He tells her, "I'll give you anything you want," probably thinking of clothes, money, or whatever teens in Galilee liked. But the girl's mother—who also happens to be the king's wife—hates you and instructs her daughter to ask for your head on a platter.

How would you respond? Would you doubt that everything you'd said or believed was true, or would you totally trust Jesus? John had some questions.

John the Baptist, who was in prison, heard about all the things the Messiah was doing. So he sent his disciples to ask Jesus, "Are you the Messiah we've been expecting, or should we keep looking for someone else?" Jesus told them, "Go back to John and tell him what you have heard and seen— the blind see, the lame walk, the lepers are cured, the deaf hear, the dead are raised to life, and the Good News is being preached to the poor. And tell him, "God blesses those who do not turn away because of me" (Matt. 11:2–6 NLT).

John had been telling everyone how to follow Jesus. He didn't care if the world thought he was insane. He pointed everyone to the Savior. Yet when things got scary, he had doubts.

What was Christ's response? Anger? Frustration? No. Jesus says gently, "Go tell John he got it right, how you've seen me in action. All of the things he was waiting for are happening. Stay strong. Don't give up."

I believe God included this story in Scripture because He wanted us to know that even those who seem to have the most faith have questions and doubts. Asking is a part of learning to trust a God we can't see or touch. In the end, John trusted the words of the Lord. He just needed a reminder. Our kids may have always had the right answers, but now, they need to know they belong to Him.

Yes, questions may push at the edge of their minds well into adulthood. Let's teach them that running away from God only produces more confusion, but seeking Him out will always bring peace.

Beauty in ACTION

1. What doubts or hard questions about faith has your child expressed?

2. How do you feel when these questions or expressions of doubt arise?

3. Do you ever find yourself avoiding your children's struggles with faith because of your own?

4. List two things you can do to help your kids spend time daily getting to know God.

···One Bite for Today···

Today, have an honest conversation with your kids about their relationship with the Lord. Let them talk openly so you can see the areas in which they are struggling and know how to pray.

Chapter 9

"They're So Insecure!":
When They Forget Their True Identity

"Please don't post that picture." Bethany was looking over my shoulder at my phone. We had just had a great day and I was about to post the selfie on social media we took together.

"I love this picture. What are you talking about?" I looked at her quizzically.

"Look at my chin, it juts out," she grumbled.

Since she has my strong jaw line, I really didn't see an issue. "You look gorgeous, and we were having so much fun here," I pleaded.

"Please don't, or can you just not tag me so no one knows I'm in it?" she implored.

This isn't the first time we've had a conversation like this, and I'm certain it won't be the last.

· Nothing but the Truth ·

My kids were adorable, wonderful, and confident as small children. We've spent time since they were young telling them they're made in the image of God and helping them reflect on the power of that truth. Over and over, we've attempted to let them see what it means to find their identity in Christ. We can never be perfect, but He is. We pull truth from Scriptures like Genesis 1:27, Psalm 56:8, Psalm 139, Isaiah 49:15-16, Zephaniah 3:17, Matthew 22:36-40, John 15:16, Galatians 3:26, Ephesians 2:10, and Romans 8:31-39.

The soundtrack John and I have repeated over and over for our kids goes something like this: "You are enough because Christ is enough. You are a precious and beloved child of the Creator of the universe. You are the Creator's created, made in His image to be His reflection. You are on the greatest mission known to all mankind: to love God with your whole self, love others as you love yourself, and share the good news of Jesus Christ with the world. But sometimes we can get so focused on the mission we are on for the Lord we can forget the mission He is on for us: to love us with an everlasting, steadfast love. This love is the most powerful force in the whole world.

"Let me tell you what that love thinks of you. You are fearfully and wonderfully made. This means God made you intentionally to be who you are, to do the good works planned for you long ago. He made you amazing both inside and out. You are entirely His workmanship, and He thinks you're awesome. Through faith you are His child, the child of the King of all kings. He chose you and appointed you to go and bear fruit. He loves you so much that whatever you ask in the Father's name, He will give it to you. He hears your voice. He knows you and loves you, not in spite of who you are, but because you are His.

"On those days when you feel inadequate and like you are not enough, remember this. He cares. He tracks all your sorrows and collects all your tears. He is with you and cannot leave you. He is the mighty warrior who saves you, He delights in you, and He rejoices over you with singing. There is nothing in this whole world that can separate you from His great love, absolutely nothing at all. If your God is for you, then who can be against you? He can never forget you. As a matter of fact, your name is written on the palm of your God's hands.

"Never forget that your heavenly Daddy is proud of you, not because of what you do for Him, although that matters, too. He sees your faithfulness. Your obedience to show up on the days you would rather not, to follow His footsteps and do what others ignore matters. Your listening to His voice and going where He goes matters, too.

"Remember, you love because He loved you first. Not for what you do, but just because you are His. You're enough always, because He is enough."

We tell them these truths while looking them in the eye, when we're walking, riding in the car, sitting in front of the television, at the park, anywhere and everywhere, as much as we can. As a kid, I struggled with my own self-esteem. In grammar school, my big blue eyes led to my nickname, "Bug Eyes." In high school, when everyone was wearing Jordache jeans (the eighties version of skinny jeans), my body shape didn't lend itself to them. So at a size 4, I thought I was overweight and built wrong. "You talk too much" and "You're too bold," people told me. I took all these things to heart and spent way too much time trying to be different instead of embracing my true identity.

I never wanted my children to have the nasty creature "Insecurity" creep into their hearts.

· Pack of Lies ·

But it happened anyway. I hate this insidious monster. We can blame it on the media. Girls are told to be more beautiful, skinny, talented, tall, tanned, and toned. Boys are told to be strong, muscular, handsome, and popular. And how do they deal with the push and pull between not being enough and being too much? There are documentaries that describe the way media is affecting our young men and women and what they think of themselves.[27] Self-esteem is such a huge struggle for this generation that large corporations like Dove spend thousands on awareness campaigns and methods to combat the problems surrounding it.

We can also blame it on words spoken to and around our kids. When your so-called friends are the ones who tell you your clothes are ugly or your overbite is too big, you wish you could hide away forever. Those closest to our children should lay the foundation for the beautiful way they can see themselves in God's eyes. When those they trust most miss this, teens come away wounded and try harder to fit into the norm.

Yes, the monster crept in and one day, and my children forgot to see themselves through the eyes of Christ. They became more focused on what they aren't than what they are. So here we sit, looking at a selfie, over-analyzing our chin, and forgetting what Jesus thinks of us. As a parent, I think the self-esteem issue may be the most exhausting part of raising kids this age. Our children need constant approval, they need to hear over and over that they are loved, and yet it never feels like enough. The issue is not that we aren't doing enough, but that they're trying to figure out who they are. As children, they accept what others tell them. But adolescence is marked by questioning.

John and I feel like we have circular conversations with all of our kids. Caleb never feels he is growing fast enough, Bethany feels the pressure to be perfect, and Kaleigh feels like she isn't good at "anything." No matter how many times we've read the Bible with them, prayed, and said, "You are loved just as you are," they don't hear it. These conversations happen every single day. They say something like "Mom, do you think I'm good enough (at a sport, in appearance, etc.)?" And John or I (or both) repeat the soundtrack described above. Then we read the Bible together, direct them into Christ's truth, and reaffirm them. But tomorrow—or later that day—we'll have the same conversation. I don't understand why, but then again, I have the same issues believing the truth about who God has made me to be.

Too often, teens hold their identity up to the wrong mirrors. The world around them screams, and although we tell them how powerful it can be to stand out, all they want is to fit in. This is where we come in. We have to keep coming back with affirmations of truth, much as we did when they were younger. They need us to speak life into their souls as a reminder of who God calls them to be. And this can be difficult, because it can seem as though they don't absorb what we say and seek affirmation from others instead.

· Under the Influence ·

But it's not that our kids don't need to hear from us. Instead, they need additional voices that speak honestly about who they are. We shouldn't step aside or stop talking but help them discern who the other voices in their lives are.

Now, let me be clear: I'm not talking about encouraging our children to people-please or seek the affirmation of others to help them feel better about themselves. Instead, they need to get beyond what they believe is "just Mom and Dad's opinion" about who they are and hear the truth of the person God knows them to be.

The other day I asked each of my kids to name five people who have been the biggest influencers on their faith up to this point. My husband and I made the list, along with teachers, coaches, mentors, their youth pastor, and family friends. Each made it for different reasons. What was interesting was that each child had someone in their life who rarely (if ever) talked to them about Jesus but at the same time modeled a way of living they desired to emulate.

Although their youth pastors did make the list, those selections came less from the sermons they gave and more from the one-on-one conversations and relationships built. And the people we look upon as professionals were not at the top of the list.

My pastor and I were discussing this, and he said his own son's list would include his parents, grandparents, and a businessman he had worked for. He said, "I think they expect those in the pulpits to know about God and teach them foundations, but they also want people who show them how to live. We're necessary, but in a different way."

My son in particular had an interesting perspective. He has had many football coaches, who, although not all professing Christians, have shown him Christ-like attributes. They've taught him teamwork, the value of giving his best, and how to use his strength for the greater good. None has ever put him down or yelled in his face. Instead, they've taught him how to work with others, have integrity, and improve with each game.

One family friend stood out to him because he's a creative type. Another on my son's list is a hip-hop artist who's also in full-time ministry as well as a great husband and dad. What Caleb loves about our friend Proverb, though, isn't this man's fame, but that he makes music because he loves it. He also used the word *servant* to describe what he loves about this guy.

Two of my kids named the same literature teacher, not because she taught Bible but because of the way she quietly shines her faith. And one Bible teacher did make the list. He knew so much about Scripture he inspired my daughter to want to know more as well. She still speaks about him with respect almost four years after sitting in his class.

As you can see, our kids are being influenced more than we realize by the adults who surround them. We don't know who will help instill in them a love of learning or let them see an example of how they want to live, so we need to pay attention to the adults who come in and out of their lives. Who are their coaches, teachers, and mentors? With whom do they have deep conversations with about their faith? Whom are they watching, and what do they see? I also realized there were only three people out of the nine that John and I had any say in: our friend and the two of us. Everyone else came into their lives because school or a sports team put them there.

Finally, every kid wants people they can ask the hard questions to, not in place of, but in addition to their parents. They need to be able to see and wrestle and think, "That person lives out their faith in a way I want to look like." Let's make sure we trust what they're saying.

John and I have had conversations with coaches, mentors, teachers, and yes, even the youth pastor letting them know our kids are struggling to grasp their identity in Christ. Each one we've approached and asked, "Could we collaborate on a plan for my child?" has been delighted to support us. I've said on more than one occasion, "I'm not looking for you to do my job, but I do need some help." We trust these people and the advice they'll give our kids.

However, we've also steered our kids away from some adults. These aren't bad people, but those who tend to offer directions and opinions that don't match the truths of God's Word. Remember, the goal is to surround our kids with those who will direct them to the Lord and His thoughts about them. He's the only one who can truly convince us of our worth. This has grown into a larger life lesson of how to filter the words of others and whose lives deserve a place of honor in terms of following their thoughts and actions. We must direct our kids to model themselves after Christ and to emulate those who reflect Him.

· Friend or Foe? ·

Adults are one thing, but what about peers who pull our kids down? These relationships can prove much more difficult to navigate.

Every youth believes they're alone in the piranha pit of adolescence and awkwardness. And any of them will say they are the only one who feels the way they do. This, of course, translates into near-continuous friend drama. One day two kids are besties. The next, they're spreading lies behind each other's backs. On top of that, every parent can identify one kid in their child's friend group whom they'd love to see go away. Maybe this kid offers regular criticism in public or private. Maybe they put their own agenda first. Maybe they don't seem to like your child, and you wonder why they keep ending up together. They may not be a bad kid, just someone who doesn't provide a healthy friendship.

When my children come home from time spent with friends like these, the mama bear protector in me comes out. I want to handle this in un-Christlike ways: letting them punch the offender or point out their acne. Yet I can't tell my kids to treat others with respect, to love others as you love yourself, and then direct them in the ultimate put-down. This is why we must help our kids navigate acquaintances, friends, frenemies, enemies, and bullies during these years. They'll encounter all of these people but shouldn't give them all the right to speak into their lives.

Our kids will have their largest number of interactions with *acquaintances*. They call them friends, but that's not what they mean. They're the people on a team who are "nice" or might share a joke with them in class, the ones who offer a pencil when theirs breaks. Acquaintances help our kids feel included. But sometimes, our shyer children have a hard time finding these people. Our kids need to have and *be* acquaintances. There are kids in their school, teams, or practices who feel isolated and need some kindness. Junior high and high school are hard enough, so encourage your kids to let them know they don't have to go it alone.

A friend of mine uses the term *safe friends* to describe a small group of people with whom our kids are always safe. They may have disagreements, but they always have their back and best interests at heart. They both celebrate and cry with you. They aren't perfect, of course, but when they cause an offense, they resolve things. Bethany has a friend who, not long ago, blurted out words that hurt her feelings—but she came back the next day and apologized. That makes her a safe friend.

Frenemy is a made-up word that might seem like a joke, but frenemies do exist: people who pose as your child's friend, but aren't. Like candy with a toxic coating, they're not safe. They abandon your kids in their time of need, criticize them when they're not around, and ask them to put themselves in situations that make them feel uncomfortable. In our home, we sometimes we call these "unsafe friends."

One of the greatest lessons we can teach our kids is how to recognize the difference between a friend and a frenemy. We don't have to tell them never to speak to these people; however, they should spend most of their time with safe friends and learn not to give the others a voice in their lives.

Enemies are not necessarily bullies. In fact, *enemy* may be too harsh a word for the kids ours don't like or, more accurately, who don't like them. It's important to teach our kids they don't have to like everyone, but they should treat everyone with respect. They must learn to navigate relationships, even those with people they don't get along with. Can they avoid them? Sit on the other side of the room? Kill them with kindness when they give them the stink-eye? Help your kids know how to properly interact with people who rub them the wrong way.

I would be remiss if I didn't touch on the topic of *bullies*, who can do a lot of damage in the heart of a child. As a child, I was bullied so much about my sensitive nature that I still remember the day I went into a school bathroom stall and vowed I would never cry in front of another person again—and I didn't until I was almost twenty-five years old. It took me years to embrace the fact that my tears were a sign of compassion and not weakness.

So yes, bullies cause problems, but we often incorrectly define them. Not every frenemy or enemy is a bully. Someone your child doesn't like much doesn't qualify. In this day of bully prevention, we need to help our kids identify the true bullies and even see if they might be one themselves.

Bullies create an ongoing situation that causes a child to feel threatened or unsafe. A bully is not someone who says, "Your pimples are ugly" one day or has no filter. A bully is the person who laughs in your child's face about their pimples so often that they don't want to go to school anymore. Help your child watch for bullies and make sure to intervene if they encounter one. Bullying, in fact, is one area in which we should never be afraid to help out our kids. No matter how old our kids are, we should be at the school, talking to the staff, interacting with the bully's parents, and stepping up in every way.

· Moment of Truth ·

At some point, I had to admit that saying, "You should believe God made you amazing" didn't fix it. I had to be honest with the way my kids were feeling about themselves. Acknowledge your children's feelings, yes, but make sure to let them know these feelings may not reflect reality. As we help them surround themselves with voices of truth, we also have to tell them to keep going before God to obtain His perspective about who they are. We have to teach them how loudly the voice of insecurity screams and that sometimes, others who buy into those lies will say things that hurt.

It's a balancing act: not giving them an over-inflated sense of self while not allowing them to get stuck in a downward spiral of feeling bad about themselves. Good days will happen. Not long ago, Kaleigh's drama teacher pulled her aside and asked her to try out for the school play. "You'll be awesome on stage, and I would love to see just how incredible you'll be," she told my daughter. Those powerful words lifted her up.

The good days are the perfect time to hit our children with extra doses of what God thinks of them. On these days we can be proactive instead of reactive, and that's beautiful.

What movies do we love the most? The ones where the plain Jane discovers underneath her average appearance is a beautiful princess. Of course, she was gorgeous all along, she just needed some help to reveal it. Never forget that the beneath all the insecurity and awkwardness lies the child you love. We can't undo the tall tales the world will tell, but we can teach our kids how to unravel them. Our goal is always to create a safe place where they can share how they feel about themselves and—have I said it enough?—point them back to the truth.

1. In what ways have you seen insecurity affect your children?

2. Ask your children which people have most influenced their lives. List the names below.

3: List the various friend relationships in your child's life below. If you have more than one child, you may want to create multiple lists.

   a. Acquaintances

   b. Safe friends

   c. Frenemies

   d. Enemies

4. Has your child dealt with bullies? How did it affect them?

5. List two things you can do to help your kids navigate relationships in a healthier way.

Chapter 10

Avoiding the Avalanche:
So Many Parenting Decisions at Once

On a recent flight, the gentleman sitting next to me and I got into a discussion about our kids. Turned out we both had boys about the same age. He was telling me about a game I'd never heard of that his son played on his phone. His response was, "Well, you probably don't really know what your son plays anyway; it's not like we can keep up." The discussion continued to books as both of our boys liked a similar series. I asked if his son had ever read a specific title and his response was, "Oh, he reads things so fast I can't even keep up with that either."

The undertone of our conversation was that it's impossible to stay ahead of the pace at which our kids absorb information. I didn't want to be disrespectful and say, "No, we know everything that goes onto our kid's devices, and we check them often." This man was overwhelmed by all the decisions we encounter as parents, and his approach was to let his son run headlong into our digital world.

· Media Madness ·

I think media is the area where parents can feel the greatest generation gap. Our children have always known what it's like to have information at their fingertips. Not long ago we were at the Smithsonian Museum in Washington, D.C., and a Sony Walkman was on display. You know, the cool, bright yellow sports model. When I was in high school, we used those on the go to listen to cassette tapes or the radio, especially during exercise. This was our idea of technology. But today's digital world moves quickly, and it feels like we can't keep up. Our kids have more exposure to information more quickly than ever before.

In addition, social media has completely changed the way we interact. We can share any thought that breaches our mind in seconds flat and then make the decision on how we want to share it. If you want to ramble, put it on Facebook. If you can keep it to 140 characters or less, use Twitter. If you take a picture of it, post it on Instagram. If you need it to disappear quickly, use Snapchat or stream it live on Periscope. By the time this book is six months old, the rules of online posting will have changed. A year or two after its release, someone might laugh that no one ever uses Facebook anymore.

Many of us prefer to interact through texting instead. It's quick, easy, and we can do it while engaging in another activity. The upside is that our kids can deal in awkward conversations with some protection against instant reactions. The first boy who liked Bethany texted her. She came running into the kitchen yelling, "What do I do?" We could talk it out and help her script an appropriate response.

The downside to any of these modern means of communication, though, is that sharing our thoughts can hurt us or others. Our children look to see who follows them on whatever forum they use, and they evaluate their worth based on who likes or doesn't like a particular post. In addition, all these online mechanisms give us the ability to reinvent ourselves. We've become more connected to each other while disconnecting from ourselves. With the rise of technology, we often present our ideal selves more than our real ones. This would be fine, except our brains don't perceive that others are doing the same thing. We've also become a society that spends less time living in the moment and more time thinking about how we can share it.

The desire to connect with others isn't wrong. It's natural. Our God made us for relationship with Himself and with other people. Jesus came to earth so we could interact and have a relationship with Him. The key to helping our kids manage technology is learning what they're using, keeping up with the ever-changing landscape, and knowing when to shut it off.

· Setting the Standard ·

We haven't even begun to touch on the impact of movies, television shows, or music on our kids. If you have a child who loves to read, be aware, as they start reading books labeled "Young Adult," that many are filled with cursing, violence, and sex. I think the reason so many of us stop tracking what our kids are watching, listening to, and reading is that we're like the dad I met on the plane. We feel it's too hard to keep up. One article says we need to clamp down and make sure we know everything our kids are doing, and another tells us we need to give them more freedom. One friend explains why his teen children aren't allowed to watch anything but G-rated movies, and another watches shows with her kids that we find wildly inappropriate.

Where do we begin? As we did with the mission, vision, and values of our family, we start with two things: telling the truth about who we are and keeping the end in mind. The avalanche hits hard on our decisions about technology because there are so many of them—all day, every day. Each of us has different convictions about the way we use our phones, our online connections, what we watch, and what we listen to.

I can have the tendency to be overly attached to my phone. I like the ability to search the answer to any questions right away and stay connected to the world at any time. On the other hand, our family doesn't have cable, and we're careful about what we watch. John and I are both visual people, and if we see something once, we replay it over and over in our minds. I can't handle cursing, gore, or sex. For this reason, John and I don't watch R-rated movies, so that means our kids don't either. Lyrics are important to me when it comes to music, and I'm picky about the songs I listen to.

As parents of teens, we don't have the freedom to adopt a "Do what I say, not what I do," attitude. Our kids are too busy watching us, and this generation is marked by a hunger for truth and authenticity. Let's not hide behind walls that say, "Live this way" while we live another. And of course, we should set standards for ourselves that match age-appropriate guidelines for our teens.

A few years ago, John and I loved the popular television show Parenthood. When we first started watching it, our kids were too young to ask about it. But as they got older, they wanted to sit with us when we watched. We said no, not because of the storyline but because the show centered around people in their thirties and forties and their interactions as a family. So we watched it, and our kids did not. Yet there did come a point when we woke up and realized there wasn't anything we watched that our kids couldn't also. That's when John and I took the position that our family rules should be the same for us all. The way we approach social media, music, and everything connected with technology is consistent for our entire family.

· Whatever Is Pure ·

You may decide this doesn't work for you. You may have a guilty pleasure show or genre of music in which you still won't allow your kids to partake. However, the key is to be honest with whom you are and what you will watch. This helps reduce pressure as far as helping your kids make the right decisions in all these areas.

Remember, everything that goes into our children's eyes and ears goes into their heads, which seeps into their hearts. If we focus on the people we want our children to become, we'll see ourselves as instilling life skills they can apply as the landscape continues to change. Look back at the vision you have for your children and remember who you want them to become.

What they watch and how they use media genuinely shapes our children for the future. It's easy as parents to think of this part of their lives as only a phase. Sure, watching the Disney Channel shows might be a phase, and the latest video game craze may fade out by the time they become adults. But thinking about what they give attention to shouldn't be a phase, and this is where the topic of purity begins. Too often we wait for our children to get to what we think is the right age before we address it. But purity is not solely about sex. Philippians 4:8 explains it: "Finally, brothers and sisters, whatever is true, whatever is noble, whatever is right, whatever is pure, whatever is lovely, whatever is admirable—if anything is excellent or praiseworthy—think about such things."

This is our number-one guiding factor when we talk to our own children about anything they watch, listen, or engage with. Purity begins with the heart. The question we ask is, "Will this bring you closer to Christ, take you farther away from Him, or neither?" If we help our children see their lives through a lens of drawing closer to Christ rather than a set of rules, we'll have equipped them to make wise choices for the long haul.

· Game Plan ·

You would love it if now I went into detail outlining the right and wrong, yes and no of what to do for our kids in this overly connected digital world. But the best way to start is to be proactive as opposed to reactive. You as parents need to have a plan of how you will approach everything from devices to video games. If you want to know what's popular right now, ask your kids. I'm not afraid to admit that I have no clue, and my children know all the words to a song before I even have a chance to hear it on the radio.

My well-meaning parents wouldn't let me listen to pop music when I was in high school. I guess they intended to protect me from the eighties. It didn't work. I can still recall sneaking into my room and putting on headphones to listen to the radio. But I want everything in the open when it comes to my kids, so we talk about music and media a lot. As far as staying up with things, online search engines are your best friend. I'm always looking up the meaning of a song, the content of a show, or the deeper subjects of a movie. A friend suggested that checking the top ten most-downloaded phone apps will also help us know what's popular. If we inquire about what our kids' friends like and also do a little research, we'll find a treasure trove of information. When we stay up on these sorts of things, we're entering our children's world, and they love it.

The rule with all of our children is that devices must be used in the open, and any of us can check anyone else's device at any time. Yes, I will allow my children to search my usage history whenever they choose. They do know that sometimes I will ask them not to look at a text stream if it contains sensitive information only meant for me. I won't say this always works seamlessly, but open doors help keep things from being hidden.

When Kaleigh was in seventh grade, we opened her door to find her huddled in the corner with her tablet. At first I was livid that she had broken the closed-door rule and positive she was watching something she should not. "You know the rule, the door needs to be open," I said firmly. "Now, what are you watching?"

Fear rose on her face, and she didn't want to show me. "You know the rule, what are you watching?" I inquired again.

"My friend wanted me to see this—it wasn't my idea." Well, it turned out to be episodes of *My Little Pony*. Kaleigh was mortified to be caught watching this babyish show, but her less-mature friend had implored her to catch up on a few episodes, and Kaleigh was being a good friend.

· Techno-Basics ·

Before they can download an app on their phone, our kids know we check texts, usage history, and have accountability systems in place. We have one television in the house, and it's in our living room. This encourages us to watch shows together and also gives us a constant knowledge of what's on. Most of all, we interact often about what we're all watching and listening to.

Early on, our kids would say, "You don't trust me" when we checked their online activity.

"It's not you I don't trust, it's everyone else," we told them. Then Caleb got caught up in a group text gone awry. He and a group of boys were finding silly pictures online and sending them to each other. John was looking through the string when he inquired, "What's this one picture here?"

Caleb said, "We said we'd find a picture of someone being stupid, so I found that guy smoking."

John pressed deeper. "What's that hanging out of his mouth?"

"Oh, it's a cigarette."

"Umm, buddy, that's not a cigarette he's smoking. That's something else entirely."

Caleb's eyes went wide. "He's smoking drugs in that picture?" He was mortified. "What if one of the boys' parents sees this? What'll they think of me?"

He has never again fought us about checking on his devices. This is not about trust but accountability. One of our roles as parents is to help guide our children in making right decisions, and being aware of their media use is a part of that. Now that we have this habit in our family, a new song will come on, and one of our kids will say, "Hey, I have the lyrics here. Let's take a look."

Hebrews 3:12–14 (NLT) puts it this way:

Be careful then, dear brothers and sisters. Make sure that your own hearts are not evil and unbelieving, turning you away from the living God. You must warn each other every day, while it is still "today," so that none of you will be deceived by sin and hardened against God. For if we are faithful to the end, trusting God just as firmly as when we first believed, we will share in all that belongs to Christ.

As parents, we hold our kids accountable to learning how to live in the Lord. Jesus loves us so much that He doesn't want anything to cause us to turn away from Him—but not because He wants us to live a boring life. He puts boundaries in place for each of us to keep us safe. No, He may not say, "Thou shalt not use Twitter." If we continue to approach boundaries as tools that keep our kids on the right road and help them learn what is safe, our kids will usually understand why we make the decisions we do.

· Unplugged ·

More and more studies are emerging about how we use our phones and mobile devices.[29] Some suggest that having our phones plugged in next to the bed affects our ability to slip into a deep sleep.[30]

Others say that our inability to go more than a few seconds without something to look at squashes creativity.[31] The reality is that we're always connected, and many of us are hooked on electronics more than we like to admit. We can all agree that we can't "read" tone in an email or text message, and feelings can be hurt unintentionally. Sometimes we judge each other in the way we present ourselves online. If we're having a bad day, we may put up a picture or post, fishing for someone to validate us. We have to help our kids know what connections are real and what is healthy when it comes to online usage and media interaction. At times, we all have to find ways to disconnect from our devices and connect with our loved ones in person.

A remake of an older movie, *The Secret Life of Walter Mitty*, contains a powerful scene that captures this truth. The movie is about a man who had to change his dreams for responsibility. Through a series of events, he ends up searching for a man who is a photographer. The main character, Walter, finds the photographer, Shawn, in the Himalayas trying to get a photo of a ghost cat (snow leopard). Shawn has been sitting for days waiting to capture this elusive animal. But he never takes the picture. Instead, he realizes that the beauty of the moment with the cat is more important than getting the photograph.

This idea captures so much of what we, along with our kids, need to realize about social networking. There are times to take the picture and times to simply enjoy the moment. In our house, no technology is allowed at the dinner table. Then, phones and tablets are shut down an hour before bed; this includes games, texting and videos. The only thing the kids can do on their device is read, and at bedtime phones are charged somewhere outside of their room. We unplug. And I submit to these rules, too. On family days, since I have the tendency to be over-connected, John keeps my phone for me. I know if I see the phone I will use it.

Let's remember, though, that media use and boundaries will not be a one-time discussion but an ongoing idea in our homes. Opening this dialogue has changed the way my kids look at media. They forget their phones more than they use them. I sometimes have to remind them the purpose of the phone is to call or text home after sports practices. And having only one television has taught us all how to find common ground and share.

The point is not to get overwhelmed but to keep interacting. We're working to build technology boundaries into our children's character, and this will help them handle this area with integrity when they leave home someday.

Beauty in ACTION

The idea of figuring out technology with our kids can weigh us down. The goal is to keeping the conversation happening and readjust when needed.

1. How have you seen the rise of social media affect your kids?

2. What is most popular with your kids right now in the following areas: television shows, movies, music, and social media?

3. What are the policies in your home for you and your children's digital usage?

4. How do you hold your kids accountable to staying pure with online usage?

··· One Bite for Today ···

This time, I'm going to leave you with two bites. First, have a discussion with your kids about accountability and expectations for technology use. Find out from them what they like and why. Second, clearly post your expectations for what they watch, hear, and do online. Don't react out of fear. Remember, this is just one more step in helping them grow into amazing adults.

Chapter 11

Too Busy or Not Busy Enough?
Figuring out a Schedule
That Fits Your Family

C an I share a dirty little secret? I don't like sports. Let me
clarify. I have no interest in watching sports of any kind—
professional, college, or local. Don't get me wrong. I like
to be active and I adore the outdoors, but nothing competitive that
involves a team.

· Good Sport? ·

My lack of interest in sports may come because growing up, sports
were never part of my family culture. I cannot recall my father
ever, I mean ever, turning on athletics on a weekend. My mom has
always enjoyed the hype behind a professional team more than the
actual game. Or my disinterest could be because I am literally the
most uncoordinated human being I know.

John, on the other hand, always played sports and loved
watching them as well. He was born into a family that had strong
generational allegiances to specific teams. On the eve of our wedding, in fact, my future mother-in-law pulled me aside and declared,
"I hope you're ready to be a sports' widow, because there isn't a
season in which John won't be watching something on a weekend
afternoon." He played soccer and Little League growing up and ran
competitively with cross-country in high school.

So of course, when our kids were small, John wanted them to

try some sports. I agreed, as long as we included the arts and other activities as well. We would go to their little games, and I would laugh at how cute they were. Yet as our children got older and their interests spread out, we made the decision to allow them to participate in only one activity at a time. On a practical level, three or four kids in the house still meant three to four different places to be at any given time.

But you can imagine my horror when they started to choose sports over the other options. This meant that I had to spend hour upon hour watching sports, engaging in sports, and most of all, caring about sports. Caleb begged us to play football, and once he finished flag, I thought it would be over—but no. In seventh grade we let him play tackle football, and that was it. Because we live in Florida, football now invades our life eleven months out of the year. This means five days of practice, games, lifting, and in the off-season, track, so Caleb can get faster and, oh yes, nights spent working out so he can get stronger. Bethany cheers for both football and basketball (don't you dare tell her cheering isn't a sport), and Kaleigh plays volleyball. So again, we have practices, games, and everything in between. Everyone gets out at different times and has different needs. I feel like all I do some days is drive back and forth to the school picking up and dropping off.

· Full Plate ·

Families make all sorts of choices when it comes to kids and activities. Once I heard an excerpt from a radio show with Dr. Bob Barnes of Sheridan House about children and sports. It was a quick clip so I can't remember if it were Dr. Barnes or someone he was interviewing, but the person talking mentioned that he and his wife had three children and only allowed one child at a time to participate in any given sport or activity.[32] They felt this gave them the ability to better control family schedules. In addition, the family could gather together to celebrate each child in their sport of choice. Recently, a friend told me about a large family who didn't want to take on the task of driving their children to various activities, so they all went running together instead. The older children trained with their parents, and they would all run anything from a 5K to a half-marathon as a crew. They believed the whole endeavor created more family time. But I can also name two sets of family friends with equally large families who spend all day Saturday at either soccer or football fields moving from game to game as each of their children plays on their respective teams. And a friend of mine told me he doesn't let his kids participate in any after-school activities. God made kids to play, he believes, and he doesn't want to feel tied to a schedule put in place by a sport.

I would honestly love it if my children didn't play any sports (or participate in an other activity outside of our home for that matter) at all. Yes, I support them. I drive to and from everything, I go to their games and cheer them on, but it's more because I love my children than because I care about any sport. Yet, I know if it weren't sportsing (the made-up word I now use to describe all athletic-based activities), it would be some other activity. Kaleigh went out for the school play after her sports season ended and now has practices for that.

When they were younger, things were a lot simpler, and our days were more our own. Then somewhere along the way, someone said, "You should start thinking about what will look good on a college application," and someone else said, "There are scholarships if your child sticks with this or that." Before we knew it, we gave up on our "one activity at a time" rule. It wasn't intentional. It was just that if two other kids were at the school anyway, why not? The rule changed to "As long as your siblings are going to be there anyway, go for it." Now, in a given week, we navigate three sports, National Honor Society, literary club, school play, youth group, youth leadership, guitar lessons, service projects, small groups, photography—and now, Bethany has a job, too.

These are just our kids' activities; we haven't even begun to talk about their homework, our role in full-time ministry, or other things we might do as a family. It may sound like a lot, but we have friends who have more kids involved in more activities. Maybe the family that runs together or my friend whose kids only play, with no outside activities, has the right idea after all.

A few years ago some family friends came to stay with us. At the time they had two kids and had just found out they were pregnant with their third. I remember vividly one day her saying to me, "I could never keep the schedule you guys do. I couldn't be you, I would be exhausted!" The funny thing is we were significantly less busy then than we are now. Yet my words to her then would still hold true: "Don't be us! Be you! Be the family you are!"

One day after teaching a workshop on women in ministry roles I was asked how I did it as a mom, wife, being in ministry, four kids and everything in between. Another woman spoke up before I could answer. "When you fill your own plate, it's overwhelming. When you let God fill your plate, you can always handle everything that's on it." That statement has stuck in the back of my mind for years now. From those of us who don't mind our kids being involved to those who don't let our children do much of anything outside of our home, we're all doing what we believe is best for our family.

When I look at why my kids do what they do, it's because they like it. We've never told them they have to play anything or even spent much time thinking about how it might help with their future. Do we hope one of these sports might translate into a college opportunity? Sure. But John and I don't want to put pressure on our kids to think this is their meal ticket. We know too many people who have had injuries in high school or lost interest before they headed to college.

We often ask, "Are you having fun?" or "Do you enjoy doing [whatever the sport is]?" If the answer is no, we require them to keep their commitment and stick out the season, and then they can be done. Kaleigh played exactly one season of junior high basketball and softball respectively. Bethany ran track one year and discovered she likes running for fun but not competitively. Creating the space where our kids know they don't have to do something forever has allowed them to figure out what they need to keep doing.

· Change of Pace ·

Although the statement about God filling our plate sounds amazing, some days, it's hard to see how that translates into a practical application. This past summer left our family totally exhausted, but not because of our kids' extra activities. As a matter of fact, we all worked in some aspect of our ministry together every day. It was nice that we all got in the car together in the morning and left together later in the day. Sure, there was football (seriously, there's always football), but on a scale of one to ten of our typical running to and fro, last summer was maybe a four. However, the ministry ran us from morning until late into the evening almost six days a week because of the way we were serving. As a matter of fact, Caleb was recently asked if there is anything he doesn't like about his parents being in ministry. His answer? "The summer is too busy." Yet, this is also the job John and I get paid to do, so it wasn't as simple as telling one of our children, "You need to quit this."

There are times when life isn't as simple as deciding whether or not our kids participate in an organized activity that makes our lives crazy. To be truthful, I have more than one full plate, and some days, I don't know how to get rid of some of the excess. It can be easy to use my kids as an excuse when what really needs to happen is a solid assessment of where we are as a family.

I've learned that family life rolls in seasons, just like sports. I think it's less about busy or not busy and more about who we are and what we can handle at the moment. If we're in the middle of tragedy or crisis, we have to trim something, so we cut down our to-do list. Yet as the day-to-day, moment-by-moment things crop up, we may have to take a solid look at putting some order into our lives just to regain sanity. This past summer, we sat the kids down and told them we had to be all in with ministry as a family. There weren't many hours in the day to do anything else, so we would take on some things, but not all. This is where having our family mission, vision, and values in place again proved valuable. We also took into account the individual personalities of each family member. Bethany loves to move at a million-mile pace, Caleb needs downtime, and Kaleigh is a mixture of both. John needs a lot of time away from the crowds, and I like to be active. When figuring out our schedule and activities, we have to consider all these factors. What season are you in? Take a hard look at your family philosophy and at each person's involvement outside the home.

At one time, I was afraid to dig deep into our family's hectic pace. It was hard to evaluate if I wanted to slow down because we needed to or because I still don't like sports. Yet sometimes, we all began to realize our lives are too full. There are moments when we look at our kids and realize we don't know their favorite things anymore, and we sense more agitation than peace in our souls. Last night I looked at John and said, "Have I even seen you this week?" To which he replied, "No." It's our code for saying, "Hey, wait, this week has been crazy and we need to connect."

However, even when we balance our schedule, sometimes things go sideways. This week, a friend's husband landed in the hospital, so we came alongside to help with their kids. When I mention the need to reevaluate, I don't mean these unusual weeks, but the times when you look back over the past month and recognize a pattern filled with more exhaustion than energy.

That's when John and I sit down and look over our schedules. We write down everything we all do on a regular basis in the course of the week and put them in order from "Have to" to "Want to." We have to perform duties associated with our paid jobs, go grocery shopping, clean the house, do laundry, and make dinner (even when we don't want to). We have to take care of our individual responsibilities. This evaluation should be done as a family overall and then with each individual. And some of the things at the bottom of the list may need to be trimmed for a day or a time.

For example, this past week was super-busy for our family with some extra things going on at school and helping our friends as well. I usually help my parents out by cleaning their house every week. I don't have to do it, but I want to because they are older and it blesses them. However, I called my mom today and let her know it just can't happen right now. John reminded me that it's all right to be honest. Sometimes we have to say, "I can't do it." Honoring and serving my parents by cleaning for them fits into our mission, vision, and values as a family. But this week when something had to drop, I chose to change this part of my schedule.

A few weeks ago I watched as Bethany was imploding under her love for too many things. We sat down together and looked over her schedule, and it was simply too much for her and for us. Some of her activities were out of our way, and getting there while navigating two other kids' schedules wasn't working. The conversation didn't go well, and tempers began to flare on both sides. Bethany kept repeating, "I can handle it." However, the reality is that I'm her parent. Sometimes, our kids need us to step in and tell them no.

After I regained my composure and prayed about my response, I realized that as much as she wanted to prove herself to us, we're still responsible for her. I don't mean just to feed, clothe, and give her shelter. She's not out on her own yet, and we want to teach her some life lessons. We have to help her be aware of her tendency to overcommit and then break down. Like her mom, Bethany will never drop a ball, but she might have an emotional breakdown in the process.

As I went into her room, I sat on her bed and began with an apology for my anger. My desire for her to slow down may have been correct, but my reaction wasn't. Then I talked to her about the need to cut something from her schedule. She still didn't like it, so finally, I said, "Something has to go. We can help you figure it out, or you can go it alone, but it has to end. I love you, and this is why we need to cut back a little."

She told me she would like to figure it out, and about an hour later she came back with a plan of a few things that could go. She wasn't happy, but I was proud of her.

The following weekend, when for the first time in a long while she could relax, she said, "I'm glad you made me do that." And the change has already had some lasting repercussions. A few weeks ago, she came to us and told us she thought she needed to quit her job during the school year and pick it up again in the summer. Bethany had just made captain of the cheer squad, and realized that with that everything else she does, it might be good to let something go. In this case, we decided together that she could keep the job as long as she only works on weekends.

· Just Right ·

As a family we have to work hard to stay connected, so we've created some non-negotiable family times. Once a week we have pizza and a movie night, and we make all or part of Saturdays family days. Our family time ebbs and flows, but we've found it vital to stay connected and have fun together. There are times when everyone in our house might need to say no to something that might otherwise be a great opportunity. We don't want our family drifting apart into isolated islands in constant motion, and we don't want our kids growing up with this as an example. Kids imitate what we model, so we have to prioritize what we can do.

Then there are times when we have a child who needs motivation to be more involved, not less. Yet, there comes an age when each child starts to find that sport or activity they enjoy and feel good about. I can't tell you what will work for each of your children or your family. If you homeschool, the way you order your day may be entirely different than mine. If you have a child with a learning challenge, you may need to focus on something else. Each of our families is so different, and we can't even begin to have a one-size-fits-all-for-all-time mentality. It's why we have to constantly look at our schedule and see how it will work with our family at any given time.

This chapter isn't about finding the latest and greatest calendar, app either. The important takeaway is to figure out your family's "Goldilocks" moment. Remember the story of the young girl who came upon the cabin in the woods? She tried out beds, chairs, and porridge in search of the elusive "just right." Some people will say your family doesn't do enough, and others will say you have too much on your plates. But take a deep look into the heart of each member of your household. What's just right for you? Do your kids need to do less, or do you need to do more? Do you need to figure out some ways to trim out one thing so you can add in another?

For now, our family schedule still includes lots of sports. And while I may never care about the actual athletic event, I do love cheering my kids on. And that makes our family and our schedule just right.

The goal of this chapter is to assess the pace of your family and what's healthy for your kids. If you want to get control of your schedule, take time to work through the questions from the chapter.

1. What activities did you enjoy as a child? How have those affected your family's current choices?

2. Do you think your kids are overextended? Why or why not?

3. Make a list of all the activities in which your family participates. Include work, school, church, sports, lessons, and other extracurricular activities.

    a. Now, go back and separate the activities into "Have to" and "Want to."

b. Invite your children to do the same.

c. Discuss as a family the activities you may need to cross off the list.

4. What do you do intentionally to stay connected as a family? If your list looks too short, brainstorm together about some activities you might enjoy.

···One Bite for Today···

Never be afraid to continually look over your schedules and make adjustments. Make that list of "Have To" and Want To" and then figure out as a family what might need to change.

Chapter 12

"Hey, There's Life Past the End of My Nose?"
Helping Our Kids
See Beyond Themselves

When I think of a servant, the first person who comes to mind is John. I know he's my husband, but he has spent almost two decades showing me what it's like to genuinely love your neighbor as yourself. For John, serving is never about an event but about doing what needs to be done (even when he doesn't "feel" like it). He partners with me in household responsibilities. If I have sports pickup duty, he makes dinner. If I'm lying in bed and realize I've forgotten something, he immediately says, "I'll get it."

· Servant Heart ·

John also does an incredible amount for our kids. This morning, he took Caleb to school at 6:30 for a fundraiser for an upcoming trip. He makes lunches for them on the nights they have too much homework and runs to Walmart at midnight to pick up the glitter they "gotta have" to finish a project.

Although he has a leadership position, I've never heard him say, "That's not my job," when it comes to ministry. He's the last guy out from an event because he's picking up trash and the first one there to help set up. John embodies for me the words of Matthew 25:35-36, "For I was hungry and you gave me something to eat, I was thirsty and you gave me something to drink, I was a stranger and you invited me in, I needed clothes and you clothed me, I was sick and you looked after me, I was in prison and you came to visit me." He is that guy.

For years John's ability to serve has humbled me. His example has also helped me learn to think of others when I'd prefer to think of myself. He and I are far from perfect, and I know reading these paragraphs will make him supremely uncomfortable. We all know our hearts, and sometimes our desire to give doesn't align with our actions. I feel like my natural tendency to want to be the center of attention disqualifies me from any compliment. But while the rest of us are talking about what a great idea it is to be a servant leader, John's out there doing it.

· … or Not ·

This has been my children's role model since the day they were born. We've worked hard to let our kids know that serving is a life-style. It's one of our family's core values and of course, a part of our mission statement: "Love Christ, serve others." When they were younger, they wanted to help. They were the first ones to show their friends compassion, and adults would tell us what great servants our kids were. Then somewhere around sixth grade, it all seemed to end. "How can I help you?" was replaced with "Why aren't you doing more for me?"

I don't know how it happened. They had more than enough time to sit for hours looking at a mobile device, but if I asked them to help with chores, I'd committed an act of torture. Mind you, these were the same chores they'd always had. My kids, who once jumped to help me clean my mom's house, now complained loud enough to be heard in the next county. I started to worry that these attitudes would carry over into adulthood.

Of course, we made sure they had opportunities to serve other than family chores. They could always come alongside us and give time in numerous ways to the community, people, and the church. We had friends with a heart to show teens different ways people were in need, so we sent our kids their way to spend time with the elderly, build ramps for the physically disabled, and feed the homeless. We thought they might just need a little push to stop ignoring others for the sake of themselves.

Then I noticed a disturbing trend. Our kids started to see serving as another activity to participate in like sports or worship band. But this wasn't our heart either. We wanted our kids to notice the world around them, and whether serving came naturally (as it does for their dad) or was a learned behavior (as it is for me), we wanted to see them follow the second greatest commandment of Christ, "Love your neighbor as yourself" (Luke 10:27c). We wanted this to include siblings, parents, the unlovable, and the events where you go volunteer for a Saturday.

For me, the question became "How do we help our kids see there's life beyond the end of their nose?" I could tell you it's just a phase, that kids become selfish when they get to be this age. And they do. Perhaps it's because they're working so hard to swim in the sea of the hardest years of their lives. I could probably dig into a bunch of reasons why they are the way they are. However, John and I won't allow our kids to grow up being more concerned for themselves than others. And I don't think we can just throw up our hands and hope they grow out of it.

· Roadblocks ·

Let's face it, we don't live in a society that's conducive to people going out of their way for one another. Not long ago, a good friend invited us to join a new small group of families who wanted to grow together in Christ. One of the goals of the group was to be intentionally missional. We use this word in the Christian community to mean going past our own family to think about those around us and love our neighbor.

Each person in the first meeting was ecstatic to get together, and every family wanted to meet together regularly, grow in community, and reach together to the world beyond ourselves. But then we pulled out our calendars to set up a regular meeting date. It took at least twenty minutes to find a time when most of us could attend consistently. I have been in similar groups that gave up after a few minutes of trying to make it work. And it took so much energy to schedule a meeting time that we haven't yet gotten together to serve.

All this shows me that our inability to get our kids out serving others isn't just about their age but about the world we now live in. In addition, we're less connected with each other than in the past. We used to know all of the people on our street, but now, we're so busy with different activities that we may not even know the names of those around us.

Our children will each look at serving entirely differently based on their personalities and gifts as well. One may serve because it's the right thing to do, another will need constant reminders, and another may serve strangers without complaint but fail to notice needs in their own family.

· Be the Pig ·

This past summer I had a revelation in where to begin with my kids as I was leading a group on a mission trip. I wrote daily devotionals for the teens, and I remembered a story a friend told me years ago which became my theme for the week. A chicken approaches a pig and says, "We should open a breakfast place together. I'll provide the eggs, and you can provide the bacon." The pig stares at the chicken for a second and then replies, "That's easy for you to say, Chicken. For you, it's a contribution. For me, it's a total commitment."[33]

I shared this fable with the team, which included my children. In life it will always be easier to be the chicken and to make only an investment in our walk with Christ. Just like the chicken, we can give an egg (a small piece) and call it a day. It's much harder to be the pig and be all in with a total commitment.

This is true of our relationship with Jesus as well. He wants us to belong to Him completely, holding nothing back. If we back up into the two greatest commandments given by the Lord in both Old and New Testaments, Luke 10:27 sums it up like this: "Love the Lord your God with all your heart and with all your soul and with all your strength and with all your mind'; and, 'Love your neighbor as yourself.'"

In other words, love the Lord with all you have, and then love others completely. The mantra I took up both to students and to my own children was this: "It's always simpler to be the chicken. Be the pig." As a matter of fact, each of my children now owns a small ceramic piggy bank with "BE THE PIG" emblazoned on the side. When we say, "Hey, be the pig," they know exactly what that means.

If you decide to use this theme in your family, make sure your kids know the fable, because they could easily start saying "Be the Pig" as an excuse to be ridiculous. But when they get the point, it helps them grow and is a way of reminding our kids that in our own strength, we'll always choose ourselves first. Not until we love the Lord with everything we are can we truly love others. This idea has begun to resonate with my kids despite their personalities or natural tendencies to ignore the world around them.

· Attitude Check ·

Although John has done an amazing job of modeling what a servant looks like, we've realized that this is another area of constant coaching in our home. I hate to say it, but it can also be the one area where we tend to lecture the most when we shouldn't. Some days I wonder if they'll ever get it. But all we can do is continue to put the idea in front of them over and again: "What does it look like to love your neighbors as yourself, in every way, even when your neighbor is your sibling with whom you're having a fight right now?"

One of the things that changes as our kids grow older is that they can acquire a sense of entitlement. That's the heart issue we confront when we ask them to love and serve others. When they're small, they help because we're their parents and they want to be near us. "What can I do to help, Mommy?" they ask. But as they get older, we often see a shift to "What will I get from this?"

Notice our focal passage says, "Love your neighbor as yourself." We serve because God told us to, and He knows what's best for us. Our motivation should not be anything we receive in return. This is why we cultivate of an attitude of gratitude in our children.

One day when the kids were small, we passed McDonald's after a day at the beach. I decided to give them a fun treat by going through the drive-through and surprising them with ice cream. I can still recall how their looks of confusion melted to squeals of glee when they found out why we were stopping. "Thank you, Mommy!" they sang in glorious chorus.

The next time we visited the beach, of course they remembered McDonald's and inquired, "Could we stop again?"

"It's only a dollar apiece," I thought, "so why not?" Their trepidation about asking erupted into another "Thank you, Mommy!"

As time passed, we didn't get ice cream every time we left the beach, but I admit, it happened often. And instead of, "Thank you, Mommy," I would hear whines about how unfair it was whenever I drove past the golden arches. The kids seemed to feel a trip to the beach meant we now owed them ice cream.

One day, feeling agitated by their moaning, I reflected on why I bought them ice cream in the first place. Was it because it felt good when they thanked me or because I wanted to give them a gift? What was *my* motivation? This idea of helping our kids look outside themselves begins with a long hard look at our own hearts. Are we willing to be late to the office because a car has broken down on the side of the road and the driver needs some assistance? Do we help a sick friend because he needs help or because he'll tell others how thoughtful we are?

I know I can forget to be grateful for what I've received. God sent His one and only Son to die a hideous death as a common criminal although He was without sin. He came to conquer death because He loves us. I often forget to live a life that oozes gratitude for what He has done and how much He wants me to be His alone.

Like my children, I can be self-centered. I expect the Lord to take care of me, answer my prayers, and come through no matter what. Sometimes I also whine when He says no to ice cream after the beach. If I truly reflect on what my life would be like without Him, I should be on my face sobbing almost every minute of the day, but I'm not. Yet He still promises never to leave or turn His back on me. His love doesn't hinge on my expressions of gratitude. Instead, He loves me because I'm his kid. And sometimes, because I trust Him, who He is, and the way He loves, me, I forget to thank Him.

Maybe we need to take the same posture with our own children. A grateful heart begins with me, and it's the only way I can teach my kids to love others. First, I must learn how to be the pig. Then, I can work on it alongside my children.

· Event or Lifestyle? ·

We also have to remember to coach our kids into noticing others without an agenda. Respond to your brother with kind words even when it's his fault (and yes, I saw what he did). Help that person in need because they're in need. Sometimes others will say thank you and other times they won't. Sometimes we'll have a warm, fuzzy feeling when we serve, and other times we'll do it simply because it's the right thing to do.

I mentioned earlier that the goal is not a service event but a lifestyle of servanthood. We should notice the broken and hurting. We should serve them whether they live on the streets or in our own homes, whether they live in an undesirable location of the world or are our own extended family members. I've had to stop telling my kids they're selfish, even though they sometimes seem that way. This isn't about self at all. All I can do is to continue to remind them that with Christ's strength, we can learn to look past the end of our nose.

I often say to my kids, "Hey, that person needs help, let's go together." Events have their place, and I recommend you find some places your family can go together to give back to your community.[34] Brainstorm together and begin with some small gestures that allow you to get to know the people who live on the corners of your property. Another good idea is to find an event you can do as a family. A friend's family serves meals to the homeless on Christmas Day to keep everyone focused more on Jesus than gifts. Our family has served at our ministry's "Christmas Store," that gives out over 7,000 toys to struggling families annually for a number of years. Even in the midst of our busyness it remains my kids' favorite family service time. Some other things we have done as a family has been serving as volunteers at a 5K that benefits cancer patients, worked at a local food pantry to organize food for a Thanksgiving event, and helped organize a community flag football event for kids. Find something that is age appropriate for everyone in your home, and pushes you all slightly beyond your comfort zone.

· You Are Breathtaking ·

The other day I walked into a public bathroom in Starbucks and found a sticky note on the mirror that read, "You are breathtaking."

My first reaction was, "Hardly." Then I realized the power of those words. This small gesture has impacted me for weeks. Someone took thirty seconds out of their day to scribble an idea and share it with the world. What a simple way to think of others and seek to bless them. They will never know how deeply it touched me or how much I needed a reminder that I'm the Creator's created.

This is the lifestyle of thinking of others. It's a process and probably one of the hardest ways to keep pouring into our kids. I want them to "get this" today, not next year, not after several years of serving and giving and going. Yet I know they'll eventually get it—as long as we keep looking at the bigger picture of belonging to Christ and learning what it means to be His. When we cultivate service in our kids and ourselves every day, thinking of others starts to become less about what we do and more about who we are.

Beauty in ACTION

As we help our kids see the world beyond the edge of their nose, think through this idea of servanthood and what it means to you and your family.

1. Name one or two people in your own life who exemplify the word servant.

2. What does "Be the Pig" mean to you?

3. What is one thing your family can do to serve someone today?

4. How can you mobilize your kids to see the world through the eyes of serving?

···One Bite for Today···

How can you go on a random act of kindness campaign this week? Start small. Are there ways each family member can all do random things for the others and then extend that? Try going outside your home for a few days to see how you can bless people. Brainstorm ideas with your kids. Can you leave sticky notes in every public bathroom for a few miles? Carry groceries from the supermarket to people's cars for an hour? Be creative!

Chapter 13

A Different Set of Milestones
and Rites of Passage:
Moving Our Kids Toward Adulthood

I have vivid memories of so much of what my children did from birth through age ten. I can still recall the first toothless grin from each of my babies, the first time they slept through the night, used a sippy cup, ate food from a spoon, and uttered words that made sense. Bethany took her first steps in our one-bedroom apartment as she walked back and forth between John and me. I was convinced Caleb would never be potty-trained until a friend of mine reminded me she had never met an adult who didn't learn how to use the bathroom—and finally, that day came. When Kaleigh first went to preschool, I remember how shocked I was to hear that my normally babbling little girl was "shy" around new people. We were sure her teacher was describing the wrong child.

We dedicated our children to the Lord as babies, and I remember the moment at which each of them understood for themselves what it meant that Jesus is their Lord and Savior. Until they turned ten years old, the milestones for physical, emotional, and spiritual growth made sense. We could get books that explained the markers for all of the important goals from eating solids to true social interactions. It was easy to know we were building a biblical foundation that would one day lead my kids into their own relationship with Christ.

Yes, we got through all of the typical benchmarks during the baby, toddler, preschool, and early elementary years. Then we hit a stride where it seemed like the kids were simply growing older. In those years, we thought we had an idea of what would happen in the next phase of life. But about four months from Bethany's tenth birthday, everything started to change. It was like she woke up one day and the reality that she was moving from being a little kid to a tween hit her hard. She cried and told us, "I don't want to grow up." Instead of seeing all of the benefits of getting older, Bethany panicked as she looked at the changes ahead. She knew she was on the cusp of some major physical changes, but beyond that, she focused on ways she wouldn't be "little" anymore. This was compounded by having two younger siblings, who although close in age, were still considered kids.

· Inside Out ·

In many ways, Bethany's situation was similar to that portrayed in Disney Pixar's *Inside Out*. In case you haven't seen the movie, it's about a girl named Riley, who is eleven years old. Riley is a happy little girl until she has to move from the Midwest to San Francisco. The audience sees inside her head to the emotions that guide her. The personifications of joy, sadness, fear, disgust, and anger are all shown at the control center of the little girl's mind. Until the move, the leader of the feelings was "Joy," but as Riley grapples with change, "Sadness" takes over. Sadness tries to help out with Riley's memories and as she puts her hands on them, their once-joyful focus becomes clouded. In her effort to fix the situation, Joy only makes it worse.

By the movie's end, Joy learns that she and Sadness can exist together and even need each other. Joy embraces the change knowing the years ahead might bring more emotional turmoil than ever before. She'll be right there with Riley, but sometimes, she may have to share the stage with other feelings.

Does any of this sound familiar? At this in-between stage, our kids want to grow while still holding tight to everything they've known. John and I often laugh about how we both played with action figures and dolls well into our fourteenth year. What changed was that we no longer talked about it with our friends. I realized Bethany didn't know how to navigate the growing-up waters yet, so she wasn't excited about the next stage.

· Growing Pains ·

John and I muddled through, wondering how to approach this new phase, until a few years ago when we had the opportunity to interact with young adults on a regular basis. I used to think our end game as parents was just to get our kids through high school. Maybe I thought a magical transformation took place at about eighteen years old when they moved out. If they were old enough to vote and go to war at that age, they must have it together, right?

But then I started to meet students who, although away from home, didn't have basic grown-up skills like doing their own laundry, cooking a simple meal, or balancing a checkbook. I met some who didn't have basic, day-to-day problem-solving skills. And that's when I realized a mere wave of the proverbial wand wouldn't change my children into solid, Jesus-loving adults who could contribute positively to society.

When it came to growing in the Lord, something else stood out, too. As my kids matured, it seemed no one really knew how to let them take the next true step in their faith. Yes, they were being encouraged to take ownership of their relationship with Christ, but most people seemed to expect that they would just get flaky as they entered adolescence. I realized many equated having doubts with a need to start over in their walk with Jesus. Teens could become believers, but few adults expected them to own their faith.

About this time, some trends and ideas started to pop up to help us guide teens through their spiritual development. A pastor from Texas named Brian Haynes came up with a concept called "The Legacy Path" that marked major developmental milestones from birth to adulthood.[35] It starts with the end in mind and provides practical ways of helping our kids grow in Christ through major touchstones. Authors like Jeremy Lee and Jim Burns often talk about rites of passage.[36] The focus with these events is connecting

God to the natural indicators for getting older like purity talks and driver's licenses.

All of these things collided in the realization that we had to sit down and come up with some ideas of how to create a series of milestones specific to our family. We needed to make a timeline that would help our children in every area from practical to spiritual. When Bethany was turning ten, the celebration of her first decade, we knew we had to start a two-part process. The first was to pick key times in the lives of our children that we would celebrate in a special way. The second was to form a list of how-to's in the areas of both life skills and spiritual goals they would need to reach before leaving home. And of course, the goal is always to send them out the door ready to face the world and fully equipped to continue to grow. Our role as parents will change drastically when they no longer live with us and are in charge of their own decision-making. But up until then, we have to keep coaching and guiding.

· Milestones and Memories ·

We made two decisions for Bethany when she was ten, both critical in helping her learn to embrace the next step in growing up as a good thing. My parents were instrumental in what we did as we searched for an experience you couldn't participate in until you turned ten. Living in Florida has its advantages, and her grandparents decided to pay for her to swim with a dolphin. The adventure was amazing, scary, and wonderful, and allowed us to emphasize this was something she couldn't have done at a younger age. She needed to know that heading into her double digits was a wonderful, powerful time.

The second decision we made was to send her to a ten-day overnight camp with two busloads of kids from our ministry. Her older cousin was going, so we knew she would be watched over. Yet, as I stood waving as the bus pulled out of the parking lot, I started sobbing. I realized Bethany's maturing was difficult for both of us. I wanted her to be excited about what lay ahead, but I now realized the countdown clock had started. I think I cried harder that day than on her first day of school.

As the next two kids turned ten, we noticed our kids approached this age in different ways. Much of it had to do with personality, and some of it had to do with gender. Our son couldn't wait for his body to change because it meant getting bigger, stronger, and potentially faster. Our daughters, on the other hand, feared the physical changes that accompany puberty. All of the kids were petrified of what attraction to the opposite sex would mean. But each needed some help to look forward to what was coming, and creating special events for each one as they turned ten helped accomplish that goal. I can't stress enough, however, that these events don't need to be expensive, just out of the ordinary.

This is also the age we start having those serious talks about how emotions, hormones, and everything in between will start to kick in. I understand the thought process behind taking your kids out for a meal to approach this topic, but it's not a one-time conversation. In our family, we chip away at these thoughts a little at a time here and there in five minutes before bed or ten minutes in the car. This helps us start the process of opening dialogue for conversations that will happen often. Whatever we do, we must demonstrate the many benefits to growing up.

John and I also sat down and made a timeline of ages we thought might be good places to stop and give an extra oomph of celebration. Along with the tenth birthday, we identified ages thirteen, sixteen, and eighteen as perfect ages to do something special. We also realized that each child might reach certain milestones specific to them and that we should focus on ages and accomplishments separately. Bethany made National Honor Society as a sophomore, Caleb's football team won the championship, and Kaleigh made the Math Olympic team. When you make your own family timeline, remember that each child will be slightly different, and keep an eye out for what's important to them.

· Celebrate! ·

When each of our children turned thirteen, we wanted to embrace their love languages as we officially marked their entrance into the teen years. Bethany has always been our ultimate girly girl, the one who, at age three, donned a blue satin Cinderella gown and had to wear it almost every day. At age four, she would only wear the color pink. However, at age ten or eleven, our princess wouldn't wear dresses, skirts, or even a hint of coral in any garment.

As she headed toward that first teen birthday, she started to return to the little girl we knew so long ago. She realized she could wear dresses and pink sometimes, but it didn't have to be all the time. Our princess bought herself a tiara, and because of her love of quality time, we headed out to have breakfast with *the* Cinderella in her castle in Orlando.

Bethany's love of words has also been a guiding force in many of the times we celebrate her. On her thirteenth birthday, I reached out to friends and family and we made a "blessing book" of letters, poems, and quotes about what being a teen would mean.

When Caleb turned thirteen, however, he and his dad went camping over his birthday weekend. He desperately wanted to commemorate becoming a man, so they watched the edited version of *Gladiator* on the iPod in their tent one night. They spent the days fishing, kayaking, and throwing mud at each other. Caleb, who also values quality time, just wanted to be with his dad. Later in the summer, we gathered fifty Christ-focused men around a campfire in our backyard, where they spent almost four hours sharing advice about what it means to grow into a man of God.

And Kaleigh? When she turned thirteen she wanted to have four of her best friends over for a weekend full of spoiling. She loves gifts, so we made sure to shop with extra care and focus on a theme. All this attention made her feel extra-special on her special day.

As our kids are rounding the corner to sixteen, we are taking a similar approach. This past summer, we took Bethany on an adventure of celebration. We decided to create something totally unique for just her. John and I felt it was important to take this milestone to celebrate how she is growing up. We found certain local landmarks that could correlate with a specific memory we had from her childhood. At each stop she received a small gift, a few words from John and I and a new quote to hang on her wall that embodied the memory. So for example we went to a her favorite childhood playground. Here John and I embarrassed her by performing the first cheer she ever learned (at 5, "Peel The Banana"). She received a pair of sunglasses to commemorate the phase in 1st grade when she had to wear pink sunglasses everywhere, and a quote from Dr. Seuss, her favorite childhood author. Caleb and Kaleigh are now excited to see how we will tailor their upcoming "16" adventures to remember their individuality. Next on our timeline will be her eighteenth birthday and then high school graduation.

Sometimes in parenting, you adopt ideas from people you know. Instead of a high school graduation party, friends of ours threw their daughter a going-away celebration. The whole family wore T-shirts for the college she would enter in just a few weeks. They gathered friends, family, and the biggest influencers in their daughter's life. Each of our kids loved this idea to help emphasize the excitement of the next stage of life.

· Skill Set ·

Along with the celebrations for ages and accomplishments, we made a list of all the skills we wanted our children to master before they leave home. This list included practical life skills like doing laundry, buying groceries, reading a recipe and cooking, following a budget, paying bills, and dealing with unexpected issues. It also included all of the skills we talked about in the chapter about doubt. Teens need to keep strengthening their faith through studying the Bible, prayer, serving, and worship. They need life lessons about integrity, humility, admitting your mistakes and having a heart sold out for Jesus. John and I realized that although we had both learned all of these at some point, no one had pointed out their importance for our adult lives. In short, our kids needed to learn how take care of ourselves. Teaching life skills is giving them "moderate independence," I once heard speaker Kurt Johnston say.[37] We want our children to know they must remain dependent on God, to learn to ask for help when needed but, for the most part, to be able to function on their own.

I remember the first time we taught Caleb how to make a

fried egg and teaching Bethany not to put a red shirt in a washing machine full of white clothing. We don't allow our children to have a meltdown when something breaks or doesn't go according to plan, either. Yes, they can throw the tantrum (even Dad and Mom do that sometimes), but then they have to think through options for fixing the situation. After all, in real life, we can't whine until someone else deals with our problems. Instead, we stand back, pray, and check out our options. Knowing how to deal with challenges, big and small, is essential.

What does this like in practical terms? Every Thursday night, we remind Caleb he needs to get everything ready for school the next day. Fridays are football game days, so this means his lunch, school books, clothes (he's required to wear a shirt and tie), football pads, cleats, and every part of his uniform. But every Friday, something's missing.

This morning, it blew up. Caleb couldn't find a shirt he needed to wear under his pads, so he lost his ability to use technology for a week. Let me show you the life skills at play in this scenario:

Follow through on what is asked of you.
Follow directions.
Don't make excuses.
Know how to solve a problem when it arises.
Do your laundry.
Apologize when you blow up.
Pray together when everything is over.

Even an everyday situation like this includes things we want to make sure our kids learn before leaving home. Look at your own family and see what life skills you've already taught your children and which ones you still need to instill.

Our kids are growing up and each step along the way they need to hear from us that we are proud of the young women and men we see before us. In the Old Testament godly leaders like Abraham, Jacob, and Moses would often build altars or towers of stone to remember a time when the Lord did something significant in their lives. Taking the time to specifically focus on dates, ages, and skill sets are a way of remembering what God is doing in our children's lives. Soon they will be past these years and onto being grown ups. For some of our children they will marry and have children of their own. We want them to look back at their own lives and know they are passing on a legacy. Let's make sure to intentionally honor, celebrate, and see our kids grow well.

1. List all the major milestones you saw in your children before age ten.

2. Did your children struggle with growing up as they hit the tween years? If so, how?

3. At what ages and for what accomplishments might you want to have special celebrations with your children?

4. Describe some ideas of ways you could celebrate, keeping each child's love language in mind.

5. Make a list of life skills your children will need before leaving home.

···One Bite for Today···

Make a timeline for your children from now until they leave your home. At appropriate ages, place the markers and skills you want to see them have before they walk out the door. What can you start to plan right now?

Chapter 14

Pure Exhaustion:
When You're Tired of Parenting

I read that television personality Kelly Ripa said she doesn't care if her kids are her friends. Her daughter was thirteen at the time and breaking some house rules, so Ripa took away her daughter's technology.[38] Oh my, a celebrity actually parented their child. How revolutionary.

· Battle Fatigue ·

Of course we know this isn't a new concept. When our children were small, it was easy to say no to ice cream for dinner (or after the beach, for that matter.) Sure, a tantrum ensued, but we stood our ground and won the battle.

But in these tween/teen years, we often become war-weary. "I'm sorry your friend was a jerk to you." "Is it possible for you and your brother to go at least five minutes without fighting?" "Screaming has never been an appropriate way to deal with your emotions." "Your body is beautiful; don't listen to anyone who says otherwise." "What do you mean, you forgot to do your homework?"

Every night before bedtime, we deal with yet another set of grenades coming in off the front lines. Some days I honestly feel like while I'm lying there bleeding, I'm expected to be the medic, too. Why can't someone else take care of the troops for a little while?

Taking the time to be a focused parent during these years is nothing short of exhausting. There have been moments when I've fallen into bed at night, looked at John, and probed, "Are we going to make it?"

I think this stage of parenting adds extra stress because we remain afraid, just as we discussed in the first chapter, that the end will prove what a poor job we've done. Perhaps we will discover that trying hard wasn't enough after all. I love last chapters in almost any book, and Pete Wilson titles the final chapter of *Plan B*, "The Bow." He points out that the final chapter in most books is like the bow we put on a gift. It's the place where we put all the pieces of the formula together and show the reader how to succeed. For this book, you'd like me to tell you that if you add all the previous chapters together, I can guarantee you great teen years and a solid young adult.

But Wilson points out that he can't put a bow on his book because there's no formula each person can follow and expect the same results. Each of us needs to allow the Lord to work in our hearts individually. In the same way, I can't give you a formula to ensure you and your child will come out of the teen years unharmed. I wish it was that easy (believe me, I do.) "For just five easy payments of $19.99 apiece, buy this book and take this pill, and I guarantee your child will become a successful member of society."

The previous chapters have armed you with tools for the journey, but none of them can ensure these years will be easy. Remember? My hope was that you wouldn't feel alone, that you would know others are in this with you, and that you would find some fresh ideas to take back into the battle.

· A Plan—or a Person? ·

We often repeat the words of Proverbs 22:6. I love the way the New Living Translation states it, "Direct your children onto the right path, and when they are older, they will not leave it." For the better part of eighteen years, we direct our kids, and then we hold our breath to see if anything sank in.

One thing we learn from studying Jesus' time on earth was that He broke the rules and didn't follow formulas. People might have expected Him to choose disciples who were scholars and had grown up in the temple. Instead, He chose a ragtag bunch of fishermen: hotheads, doubters, and one who would betray Him all the way to the cross. The nation of Israel was looking for the arrival of a political king to save them from Rome. But Jesus came to save our souls. He not only let the lepers, prostitutes, and unclean come near, but He embraced them and made them whole. Many people thought He messed up, approached His ministry entirely the wrong way, and ended up as a total failure.

But Jesus also forgave people of their sins and brought healing on the Sabbath. He made declarations like this: "I am the way and the truth and the life. No one comes to the Father except through me" (John 14:6). In the end, the king of the Jews was captured and crucified—until, of course, He conquered death and restored our relationship with God. His was exactly the right plan; it was just unconventional. The key to everything was his relationship with the Father.

I can't stress enough: this, too, is what we have to give. The bedrock of our parenting lies in the fact that we don't know all the answers, but know the One who does. All we can do is parent from His lap, asking Him to help us do it well. Let's look once again at to the words of Deuteronomy 6:5-9:

> Love the Lord your God with all your heart and with all your soul and with all your strength. These commandments that I give you today are to be on your hearts. Impress them on your children. Talk about them when you sit at home and when you walk along the road, when you lie down and when you get up. Tie them as symbols on your hands and bind them on your foreheads. Write them on the door frames of your houses and on your gates.

In these final years our kids remain at home, it's more vital than ever that this verse become our mantra. First, we love God with everything we have. We allow Him to engrave His words into our hearts. Then we show our kids what this looks like everywhere we go and in everything we do. You've seen that through the pages of this book: in the car, during school projects, in good times and bad, when we're overwhelmed, when we feel like we're failing, when we put them to bed, and when they wake us up talking about everything (or not saying a word).

Everywhere we look, we need to help our kids see who God is and what that means. In other words, we've spent years showing our children how high and wide and deep Christ's love is for each of us. Like Jesus, when we belong to the Father, everything else makes sense.

Yes, I know what you're saying. Parenting teens this way all the time, everywhere is grueling—more draining than the first years of their lives added together. I get it. We strive to have Christ as the foundation and center. Do you recall that I've worked with teens for almost twenty-four years? So yes, I should be more equipped than most people. And I say all of this again to let you know how often I'm overwhelmed. This is why I have such a heart to walk with other parents in this same phase of life. You may think, "I can't do all the things you suggested." That's fine. Here's my charge to you.

· Parenting: Don't Pass It On ·

Dad and Mom, I know you're tempted to pass the parenting on to the professionals. Youth pastors, teachers, coaches, and all directors of teen activities hang out with adolescents all the time. Surely they know how to connect better than parents. Many people assume the younger a person is, the more they can relate to our kids. Our kids seem to want to be with these other people anyway, so let's just let those people take control of at least the difficult concepts. I urge you: avoid the temptation to pass the work to someone else. And don't you dare give up.

Chap Clark in his book *Hurt* talks about systematic abandonment. This is his belief that adolescents today feel like they've been deserted by every adult and system meant to keep them safe.[39] He would say parents are so focused on getting our kids ahead that we push for success in school and athletics. We fear we can't afford college or training, so our kids need to do something outstanding to get scholarships. Athletics used to focus on teamwork, but now, the focus is winning. So our kids feel pushed yet again. And when we parents feel inadequate, we drop them off at youth group so they can "get Jesus." That leaves our adolescents feeling like they've been systematically handed off to still more adults with agendas for success.

This is also why students often feel there are no safe adult relationships. The "post-modern family," as Clark calls it, is focused on meeting needs and working through struggles. The extended family is rare, and teens have few healthy relationships with adults as mentors.[40]

But we don't have to settle for this negative trend. Remember that no matter how many hours our kids spend with other adults, we remain their parents. Teachers, youth pastors, and coaches are not the ones who get to see the underbelly of insecurity balled in the stomach of our kids. They're not solely responsible for feeding, clothing, or housing them. They don't get up in the middle of the night to deal with their stomach flu, ear infections, or coughs. In fact, they've only known our kids for a few short years. We taught them to walk, talk, and ride a bike. We even found creative ways to overcome "corn face" so they would eat their veggies. If we haven't yet, we're the ones who will teach them to drive and deal with heartache or bullies. No matter how much our kids deny it, we still hold the greatest influence in their lives, and we're still the ones they want when their world is falling apart.

· Farmers R Us ·

Not long ago, Caleb unwittingly made a deep cut in my heart. One evening, our family was discussing the most meaningful lesson about Jesus each of our kids had learned this past year. Caleb said, "That doubting your faith isn't a sin, and that Jesus always comes through."

All right, this is good. But then came the kicker. "I learned that at youth group. It's the first time I'd ever heard anything like this."

My eyebrows raised as I tried to keep my composure. What are you talking about? What about every day we discussed this same topic with you for the past four years? What about all the times we sat and prayed with you about this? What about every car ride and bedtime when we answered your questions? What about the Scripture and devotionals we put in your hands? Have we been talking into a vacuum?

I wanted to scream all these questions at him. Instead I quietly asked, "You really believe this is the first time you've heard this?"

"Well, I don't know." As I stared in silence at my dinner plate, he followed up with "Mom, did I hurt your feelings?"

What could I say? "Yes, apparently our efforts to discuss the topic of doubt could never compare to youth group. They give one sermon, and it's amazing. We plug along for years, and it doesn't even make a dent."

That's what I wanted to say. But I had to remember that truth is making its way into his heart. And the Lord reminded me of something He had shown me years before. We tend to focus on the idea that the "harvest is plentiful but the workers are few" (Matt. 9:37b). However, we often forget about another important New Testament passage from the apostle Paul:

I planted the seed in your hearts, and Apollos watered it, but it was God who made it grow. It's not important who does the planting, or who does the watering. What's important is that God makes the seed grow. The one who plants and the one who waters work together with the same purpose. And both will be rewarded for their own hard work. For we are both God's workers. And you are God's field. You are God's building. (1 Cor. 3:6-9, NLT)

As parents, we're farmers, and that means we do more than harvest. Farmers prepare the soil. They dig up rocks and dirt and make hardened ground ready for seed. They fertilize and till. Then they plant little seeds. They water and wait—and wait and wait. They protect the baby plants from pests, weather, and the elements.

Farmers also work with others. No one can care for an entire crop by themselves. As crucial as our role is in the life of our kids, we need those extra hands who will come alongside us in the field. Our job is to look at the hearts of our children and believe that one day, they'll grow. God the only one who can do that work, and we must look with His eyes. The average passerby may see only a field of dirt, but we see something amazing.

· Top Model ·

Now think back on your own life. Were your parents your only influencers? Who were other major people who helped shape you in some way? My Grammie Leneita; my fifth-grade teacher, Mr. Barnacoat; the first pastor who hired me, Leo Suave; and my first boss in urban ministry, Lynn Ann Bogard, are ones I can think of right away. These people, in addition to my parents, taught me life lessons or showed me a skill. But at no time did they replace my parents.

If children are being abandoned as Clark says, let's help them understand the real systems that can keep them safe. Years ago, youth pastor Mike Yaconelli made a charge to youth workers. If the extended family is lacking, he said, youth workers should come alongside them to fill those gaps. Our kids don't need youth workers to be their parents; however, they may need others to serve as aunts, uncles, cousins, older siblings, and even grandparents. If adolescence is marked by the need for role models, our job as parents is to lead while surrounding our kids with voices that will support and supplement ours.

As a role model and coach, I sometimes have a hard time understanding the line between letting my kids gain independence and my own desire to remain in control. I'm so glad growth is gradual. My tendency as a parent can be to hold on tighter while they're heading down the road to more freedom.

It's been difficult sometimes to know when to allow others to speak into my kids' lives. We've been told that in the push and pull of independence, our kids will want nothing to do with us. When we set up mechanisms that open conversations with our kids, though, this simply doesn't prove true. There are also times when trusted people can come alongside us and reaffirm truths we share. I think what Caleb was really saying when he shared his revelation about doubt was, "I see now this isn't just your opinion, this is a truth I can grab hold of." Something special starts to happen when we settle in for the long haul but gather extra voices to speak into our kids. We need some extra farm hands to help that field reach its potential.

I'm thankful for the youth pastor who took a too-loud seventh grade girl with no filter and declared her a leader. For the football coach who told a young boy he would grow and was continuing to get better at the game he loves. For the pastor who saw my daughter's love for photography and not only gave her a camera but teaches her how to improve at the craft. I have tears of gratitude for those who have taught my kids skills I lack. Each of these people has reinforced ideas we teach at home: service, integrity, hard work, teamwork, creativity, respect, and loving the Lord. And when my kids have a question or want to know how to move forward, they come back to us.

Sometimes we forget that while we aren't our children's friends, we're not their enemies, either. Parenting is not about maintaining control but about the recognition that our kids still need and want parents—even when they don't act like it. They, too, know a time is coming when we won't be looking over their shoulders with decision-making rights in their lives.

In truth, the closer the time for leaving home gets, the more uncertainty both parent and child experience. Our kids no longer want to learn to dance by standing on our feet, but that doesn't mean they've stopped wanting to learn to dance.

They don't want us to be friends—or enemies, either.

They aren't looking for a hero or dictator.

They want a role model.

In your home, remember to use the word *accountability* often. Accountability lets them know they need other people to help them move in the right direction. We're always accountable to God, who sets boundaries in our lives yet allows us to have freedom of choice. No matter how old we get, we need our parents to be our parents.

So let's keep it up. Keep being the parent. Don't worry about making your kids happy. Be creative with your discipline, talk to them often, never stop praying, and know that God is bigger than we are.

Unsure what to say to your kids? Romans 12:9-21 sums up almost every lesson we need to pass on:

> *Love must be sincere. Hate what is evil; cling to what is good. Be devoted to one another in love. Honor one another above yourselves. Never be lacking in zeal, but keep your spiritual fervor, serving the Lord. Be joyful in hope, patient in affliction, faithful in prayer. Share with the Lord's people who are in need. Practice hospitality. Bless those who persecute you; bless and do not curse. Rejoice with those who rejoice; mourn with those who mourn. Live in harmony with one another. Do not be proud, but be willing to associate with people of low position. Do not be conceited. Do not repay anyone evil for evil. Be careful to do what is right in the eyes of everyone. If it is possible, as far as it depends on you, live at peace with everyone. Do not take revenge, my dear friends, but leave room for God's wrath, for it is written: "It is mine to avenge; I will repay," says the Lord. On the contrary: "If your enemy is hungry, feed him; if he is thirsty, give him something to drink. In doing this, you will heap burning coals on his head." Do not be overcome by evil, but overcome evil with good.*

And it's OK that you close your eyes and wish it was still as easy as scooping them up in your arms to protect them from all harm.

· Be the Parent ·

But have no fear. Just as our kids did with those scraped knees of days gone by, they'll overcome the pain and get back up. Sometimes, they'll take our hands and let us help. At other times, our job is to stand nearby while they do it themselves.

No, I can't give you a beautiful bow to wrap it all up. There are so many topics we didn't have the time to touch on in the short pages provided for us here. You might still be hoping for a formula that shows you how to navigate dating, college, and more. You'll fall into bed tonight and wonder if they might grow up to be on the FBI's Most-Wanted list.

If they can't remember to clean their room or finish their homework, will they ever be able to live on their own? Yes. They will. There will also be days the phone will ring and they'll say tentatively, "Dad or Mom, I need your advice." Mark Twain summed it up like this, "When I was a boy of fourteen, my father was so ignorant I could hardly stand to have the old man around. But when I got to be twenty-one, I was astonished at how much the old man had learned in seven years."[41]

Some days are just hard. Those are the ones when we'd rather focus on all the things that go wrong instead of the people our kids are becoming. But once in a while, we get a glimpse into the true beauty of who they are and will be. They do some chores without being asked. They hug us and say thanks. They work hard to do well in school. And we breathe for a second before the work starts all over again.

It's going to be OK. I promise. When you don't believe it, at least believe the Lord is bigger than all of us. He loves our kids more than we do, and He won't give up on them.

Just keep being their parent—and remember to enjoy the beautiful chaos along the way.

1. Look again at what it means to you to belong to Christ. Write a brief summary here.

2. Name three people in your life who helped shape you.

3. Name three people who come alongside you in your children's lives. If you have several children, you may want to list more than three.

4. Name one thing you will do today to keep showing up in your kids' lives.

···One Bite for Today···

Take the time to go back through this book often. Use it as a guide when you need to approach your children from a new angle. Take the time to put the beauty into action, and often. Our first "bite" was a charge to tell your children you love them. Find ways every day to communicate this same message in words and actions. Your love will add momentum to their seeing and understanding the unconditional love of Christ.

Endnotes

Chapter 1:

1   Beth Azar, "How Do Parents Matter? Let Us Count the Ways," American Psychological Association, http://www.apa.org/ monitor/julaug00/parents.aspx, (July 2000).

Other articles that discuss the importance of parental influence in the life of a child:

Bethel Moges and Kristi Weber, "Parental Influence on the Emotional Development of Children," Developmental Psychology at Vanderbilt, https://my.vanderbilt.edu/ developmentalpsychologyblog/2014/05/parental-influence-on-the-emotional-development-of-children/, (April 7, 2007).

"The Power of Parents," Royal Canadian Mounted Police, http://www.rcmp-grc.gc.ca/docas-ssdco/guide-kid-enf/page3-eng.htm, (January 6, 2016).

Sara Bellum, "Parents: How Much Do They Influence You?"

"Adolescence and the Influence of Parents." *Psychology Today*, https://www.psychologytoday.com/blog/surviving-your-childs-adolescence/201010/adolescence-and-the-influence-parents, (October 18, 2010).

Chapter 2

2   Malcolm Gladwell, *Outliers: The Story of Success* (New York: Little, Brown, 2008), 32-33.

3   Saul McLeod, "Erik Erikson | Psychosocial Stages | *Simply Psychology*." Simple Psychology, (2013). .

4   Ibid.

5   "Adolescence and the Influence of Parents," *Psychology Today*, https://www.psychologytoday.com/blog/surviving-your-childs-adolescence/201010/adolescence-and-the-influence-parents, (October 18, 2010).

Chapter 3

6   Phil Vischer, "Instill a Lifelong Love of the Bible in Your Students," 2015 D6 Conference.

7   Kate Russell, "Why Teenagers Don't Talk to Their Parents," *The Huffington Post*, http://www.huffingtonpost.com/kate-russell/why-teenagers-dont-talk-to-their-parents_b_6725700.html, (February 23, 2015).

8   Joanne Stern, Ph.D. "5 Things Every Teen Wants Their Parent To Know," *Psychology Today*, https://www.psychologytoday.com/blog/parenting-is-contact-sport/201109/5-things-every-teen-wants-their-parent-know, (September 14, 2011).

9   Meghan, Vivo. "10 Things Teens Wish Their Parents Knew," Aspen Education Programs. Aspen Education Group, http://aspeneducation.crchealth.com/10-things-teens-wish-their-parents-knew/, (2014).

10 "Inside the Teenage Brain, Interview with Ellen Galinsky," PBS, http://www.pbs.org/wgbh/pages/frontline/shows/teenbrain/interviews/galinsky.html, (2007).

11 Gary Chapman, *The Five Love Languages: The Secret to Love That Lasts* (Chicago: Northfield, 2004). You can also check out the website, http://www.5lovelanguages.com, where you and your family members (including children) can take a quick and simple test to discover your love languages.

12 Eric Pickersgill, "Removed Project," http://ericpickersgill.com.

Chapter 5:

13 Anne Fishel, "The Family Dinner Project," The Family Dinner Project. http://thefamilydinnerproject.org/, (February 18, 2016).

14 NCASA

15 Jennifer Utter, Simon Denny, Elizabeth Robinson, Theresa Fleming, Shanthi Ameratunga, and Sue Grant. "Family Meals and the Well-being of Adolescents," *Journal Of Pediatrics and Child Health*. Wiley Online Library, (October 31, 2013).

16 Lee C. Bollinger, comp. "The Importance of Family Dinners," PsycEXTRA Dataset VII (2012): 1-10. Columbia University, http://casafamilyday.org/familyday/files/media/The%20Importance%20of%20Family%20Dinners%20VI%202010%20-%20FINAL.pdf, (September 2012).

17 Lee C. Bollinger, comp. "The Importance of Family Dinners," PsycEXTRA Dataset VII (2012): Columbia University, http://casafamilyday.org/familyday/files/media/The%20Importance%20of%20Family%20Dinners%20VI%202010%20-%20FINAL.pdf, (September 2012).

18 A. A. Milne, Winnie The Pooh (E.P. Dutton, 1926).

Chapter 7:

19   Additional Resources for helping with struggling kids:

A book that touches on many topics does not allow time to truly cover every detail in depth. In his book, *Boundaries with Teens*, Dr. John Townsend does a phenomenal job of digging deep into this idea and gives practical ideas on how to approach a variety of topics that deal with discipline.

Another great book is *Different Children Different Needs: Understanding the Unique Personality of Your Child* by Charles Boyd.

Dr. Jim Burns and his ministry "HomeWord" (homeword.com) have many resources to help as well.

Chapter 8

20   Word "doubt" Merriam-Webster. Merriam-Webster, n.d. Web. 23 Feb. 2016.

21   "U.S. Public Becoming Less Religious." *Pew Research Centers Religion Public Life Project RSS*. Pew Research Center, http://www.pewforum.org/2015/11/03/u-s-public-becoming-less-religious/, (November 2, 2015).

22   Daniel Burke, "Millennials Leaving Church In Droves, Study Finds." CNN, http://www.cnn.com/2015/05/12/living/pew-religion-study/, (May 14, 2015).

23   Ed Stetzer, "The Real Reasons Young Adults Drop Out Of Church," *The Exchange*. Christianity Today, http://www.christianitytoday.com/edstetzer/2014/december/real-reasons-young-adults-drop-out-of-church.html, (December 1, 2014).

24   Lee Strobel, Robert Suggs, and Robert Elmer, *The Case for Faith for Kids* (Grand Rapids: Zonderkidz, 2006).

25   Todd E. Brady, "4 Valuable Tips on Children and Bible Reading." *4 Valuable Tips on Children and Bible Reading*. Lifeway, http://www.lifeway.com/Article/valuable-lessons-on-children-and-bible-reading, (2015).

26   Ibid.

Chapter 9

27   *#Being13: Inside the Secret World of Teens, The Mask You Live In, The Illusionists, Generation Like.*

28   ** AUTHOR'S NOTE: If you see a drastic change in your child's behavior, they may need help beyond what you can offer. Consider having them see a professional counselor who can provide tools to help them hear the truth as God says it. If your child often seems

sad or behavior is erratic, you may want to seek out professional help. Sometimes our good kids are struggling, and they may need more help than we can give.

Chapter 10

29 Emily Drago, "The Effect Of Technology on Face to Face Communication," *The Elon Journal of Undergraduate Research in Communications*, Elon University, https://www. elon.edu/docs/e-web/academics/communications/research/vol6no1/02DragoEJSpring15.pdf, (Spring 2015).

Helen Lee Lin, "How Your Cell Phone Hurts Your Relationships," *Scientific American*, http://www.scientificamerican.com/article/how-your-cell-phone-hurts-your-relationships/, (September 4, 2012).

30 Hall, Katy. "How Mobile Phones Affect Sleep (INFOGRAPHIC)," *The Huffington Post*, http://www.huffingtonpost.com/2013/02/15/phones-sleep-mobile-_n_2680805.html, (February 15, 2013).

KGW Staff. "Doctor: Cell Phones Hurt Sleep Quality," Online News Posting. *KGW*. http://legacy.kgw.com/story/news/investigations/2014/04/14/doctor-cell-phones-hurt-sleep-quality/12584984/, (February 19, 2015).

31 Jessica Stillman, "Is Your Smart Phone Killing Your Creativity?" *Inc.com*, http://www.inc.com/jessica-stillman/is-your-smart-phone-killing-your-creativity.html, (April 3, 2013).

NPR Staff. "Bored . . . And Brilliant? A Challenge To Disconnect From Your Phone." *NPR*, http://www.npr.org/sections/alltechconsidered/2015/01/12/376717870/bored-and-brilliant-a-challenge-to-disconnect-from-your-phone, (February 2, 2015).

Monica Guzman, "In Defense of Boredom: Why Your Phone Is Killing Your Creativity," *GeekWire*, http://www.geekwire.com/2015/defense-boredom-phone-killing-creativity/, (February 4, 2015).

32 Dr. Bob Barnes, President and Founder Sheridan House, "Parenting On Purpose," www.parentingonpurpose.org. Note: Dr. Barnes is a magnificent resource on parenting teens, and parenting in a single-parent setting.

Chapter 12:

33 C. P. Puri, Agile Management: Feature Driven Development (Global India Publication 2009).

34 Some places you might consider serving as a family are:
Homeless shelter
Food bank
Thanksgiving food drive

Food pantry at a local church
Soup kitchen
Nursing home
Local chapter of ARC for challenged citizens
Local library
SPCA
Boys and Girls Club
Local non-profit benefitting struggling children
Find a walk or run that supports a "cause" like cancer, or
autism awareness
The goal is to find a way that helps your children understand
service is not an "event," it is a lifestyle

Chapter 13

35 Brian Haynes, The Legacy Path: Discover Intentional Spiritual
    Parenting (Nashville: Randall House, 2011).

36 Jim Burns and Jeremy Lee, *Pass it On: Building a Legacy of Faith
    for Your Children Through Practical and Memorable Experiences*
    (Colorado Springs: David C. Cook, 2015).

    Jim Burns, *Confident Parenting* (Bloomington: Bethany House,
    2008).

    Jim Burns, *Faith Conversations for Families* (Ventura: Regal, from
    Gospel Light, 2011).

    Jeremy Lee: Parentministry.net.

37 Kurt Johnston speaking at the 2015 D6 Conference.

Chapter 14

38 Ree Hines, "Kelly Ripa Doesn't Care If Her Kids like Her: 'I'm Not
    Your Friend'" *TODAY.com*. Today, http://www.today.com/parents/
    kelly-ripa-doesnt-care-if-her-kids-her-im-not-1D80274280,
    (November 7, 2014).

39 Chap Clark, Hurt 2.0: *Inside the World of Today's Teenagers* (Grand
    Rapids: Baker Academic, 2011.)

40 Ibid.

41 Mark Twain, "ToInspire Quotes." ToInspire Quotes. N.p., n.d.
    http://www.toinspire.com/author.asp?author=Mark%2BTwain,
    (February 24, 2016).

What is **D6**?

BASED ON DEUTERONOMY 6:4-7

A **conference** for your entire **team**

A **curriculum** for every age at **church**

An **experience** for every person in your **home**

Connecting
CHURCH & HOME
These must work together!

D6 CONFERENCE
ONCE A YEAR

DEFINE & REFINE Your Discipleship Plan

www.d6family.com

ONE HOUR
A WEEK

POWER OF
PARENTAL INFLUENCE

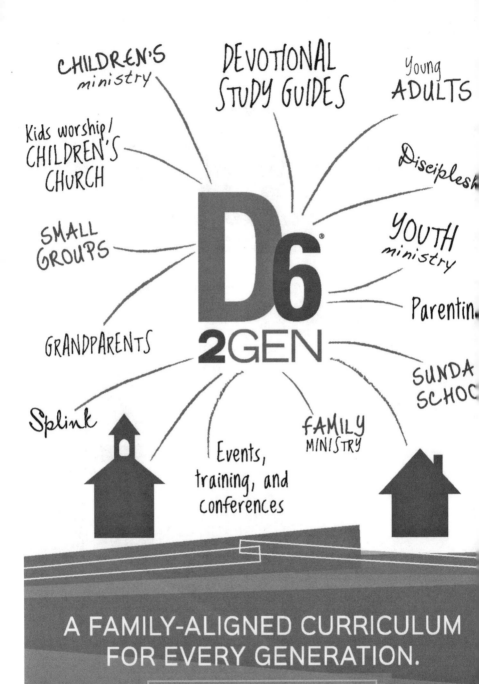

CHILDREN'S *ministry*

DEVOTIONAL STUDY GUIDES

young ADULTS

Kids worship/ CHILDREN'S CHURCH

Disciplesh

SMALL GROUPS

YOUTH *ministry*

GRANDPARENTS

Parentin.

Splink

SUNDA SCHOC

Events, training, and conferences

FAMILY MINISTRY

A FAMILY-ALIGNED CURRICULUM FOR EVERY GENERATION.

WWW.D62GEN.COM

Based on Deuteronomy 6:5-7

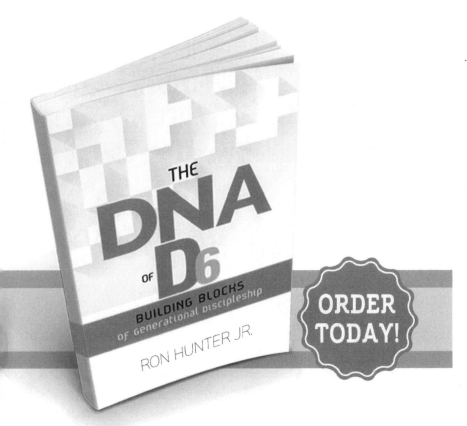